Handling Difficult People

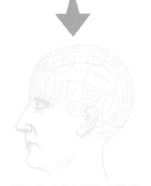

JON P. BLOCH, PH.D.

BORDERS.

Published by
Adams Media,
an F+W Publications Company
57 Littlefield Street, Avon, MA 02322. U.S.A.
www.adamsmedia.com

ISBN: 1-59337-533-6

Printed in Canada.

J I H G F E D C B A

This publication is designed to provide accurate and authoritative information with regard to the subject matter covered. It is sold with the
understanding that the publisher is not engaged in rendering legal,
accounting, or other professional advice. If legal advice or other expert
assistance is required, the services of a competent professional person
should be sought.

—From a *Declaration of Principles* jointly adopted by a
Committee of the American Bar Association and a
Committee of Publishers and Associations

Many of the designations used by manufacturers and sellers to distin-
guish their products are claimed as trademarks. Where those designations appear in this book and Adams Media was aware of a trademark
claim, the designations have been printed with initial capital letters.

Interior illustrations by Studio Editions ©1990.

*For bulk sales, contact your local Borders store and ask to speak
to the Corporate Sales Representative.*

contents

introduction

So You Know a Difficult Person?
(Who Doesn't?)

"My life would be so easy if it weren't for So-and-So."

How often do you say these very words? Or more to the point, how many times *a day* do you say them? One of the few certainties in this world is that whatever you do for a living, and whatever your family background, you will encounter people who make what you're doing so much more complicated and unpleasant than it needs to be. "Hell is other people," uttered the famous philosopher Jean-Paul Sartre, and you don't need a Ph.D. to understand exactly what that means.

Maybe you've quit a job, thinking: "Now my troubles are over—I never have to see So-and-So again." But then the next job brings some spanking new manifestation of Hell in the form of a *new* coworker or boss. The same thing can happen when you drop out of a class, religious or political group, or even a recreational activity. The *next* endeavor you undertake can become just as quarrelsome or depressing, thanks to some new person who seems determined to make your life as miserable as possible.

Maybe you've tried so very hard to change a situation with a family member whom you must keep seeing. You thought to yourself, *"Next* time I talk to So-and-So, it will be different." Only this magical "next time" never seems to come. Face-to-face in the moment, things unfold pretty much as they always have before—i.e., lousily.

Will reading this book magically transport all the difficult people in the world into a black hole in space where they belong? Will reading this book somehow fix it so that you will never again encounter a difficult person? Alas, the answer is "no" on both counts. Unless you wish to become one of the reclusive types who lives on home-delivered pizza and otherwise never connects with anyone, you simply *will* have to deal with difficult people. Even the pizza-loving recluse might encounter a difficult delivery person. And besides, you do have things you want to accomplish, and people you want to see.

So what this book can do is help you to make your life *better* when it comes to difficult people. You'll be given three basic tools:

1. A list of ten difficult personality types—arranged alphabetically—and how to spot them.

2. How you can keep your encounters with such people to a *minimum*. (No, you cannot eliminate them, but you can *minimize* your dealings with them.)

3. How you can respond to these people in ways that *improve* your ability to communicate with others and feel good about yourself. ("Improvement" does not mean perfection, but it does mean "better than before.")

Sometimes certain sayings become so overly familiar that they become clichés, and start to lose meaning. If you've ever watched a TV talk show, you have no doubt heard the phrase, "You cannot change another person, you can only change yourself." Or some variation thereof. As annoying as this phrase may seem when you are in the throes of hating someone's guts, like many such time-worn sayings it unfortunately is true. So let us make one thing clear at the outset:

You really—REALLY—cannot change another person.

It might seem frustrating—or even painful—to embrace this basic fact of life. Why *can't* your boss listen to what you have to say? Why *can't* your brother-in-law stop bragging about his golf game? It should be so simple. Maybe you've even tried to point this out to a difficult person; maybe in the moment, they even seemed to get it. But then five minutes or five months later, things are right back at square one. As another well-worn cliché would put it, "People only change when they are ready to change."

Does this mean you should never speak up when someone is getting on your nerves? Absolutely not. First of all, it is important to make your needs known to other people. And sometimes, you *can* make a difference in their lives. For example, you can probably get someone to remember that you don't like strawberries, or to no longer call you by a nickname that annoys you, or to stop asking if you watched the World Series when you are not a baseball fan. But you know, even in such small matters, things can get dicey. Even a spouse or lifelong best friend might *still* forget about the strawberries, or be unable to resist teasing you by calling you by that annoying name.

However, there *is* something you can do: **You can change your own behavior when you encounter these people.** If you find them *that* irritating, you can keep your encounters with them to a minimum. And if you must deal with them, you can change how you respond to them—both on the outside *and* on the inside.

HOW THIS BOOK IS ORGANIZED

Each chapter consists of the following parts:

➔ Clues on how to spot a given personality type

➔ An explanation of how that person got that way

➔ How to avoid that type of person

➔ How to better deal with that type of person face-to-face

You will notice that there are suggestions for both avoidance *and* confrontation. The truth is, life is not a *Rocky* movie in which you will be able to knock out difficult people every time you encounter them. (After all, even Rocky sometimes loses the fight in his movies.) Only dirty fighters win all the time, and if you have any morals and principles at all—as I'm sure you do—you are not a dirty fighter. So sometimes, good old-fashioned avoidance really is the smart thing to do. But other times, there is no reason you cannot stand up for yourself and make it known to a difficult person that you have had quite enough, thank you very much. And there are plenty of helpful ideas for how to do this.

Before we get going, one final word of caution: The difficult people described in this book are hopefully within your power to do something about. You must think so, too, or else why read this book? But some people are not merely difficult but *dangerous*—they can physically harm you or cause you to lose your job. If someone is *that* level of problem, by all means contact the police, your lawyer, your boss, your union, or your doctor.

So, without further delay, welcome to the wonderful world (ugh!) of handling difficult people—and what you can do to help *yourself.*

the big bully

CHAPTER ONE: The Big Bully is a familiar figure from childhood. This was the kid who actually *enjoyed* hurting other people—whether the pain was physical, emotional, or both. The point of bullying, of course, is to look good by making you look bad. The Big Bully appears to have power over you, and this puts him or her in a position of superiority. Plus, if you are afraid of Big Bullies, you might do things to please them. Maybe you did homework for a Big Bully, or gave him or her your lunch money. But first and foremost, these people enjoy power, and making you suffer. Some would argue that this makes them ideally suited for high-level political office—or failing that, credit card customer service.

All joking aside, Big Bullies are a serious social problem. Sometimes adults are perfectly aware of what a Big Bully kid is doing, but because it is *their* kid, or because they think getting bullied is "normal," they do nothing. Actually, life is hard enough for kids without having to face someone who fills them with mortal terror on a daily basis. No one should have to go through this. That so many people can eventually forgive their childhood Big Bullies or even laugh about it all says volumes about the strength of the human spirit.

Public awareness about childhood bullying has increased. However, it is often overlooked that the Big Bully might continue to rear his or her not-so-pretty face way beyond the schoolyard. Studies show that while many juvenile delinquents outgrow criminal activity, some become career criminals. Similarly, some childhood bullies grow into career bullies. Relatives such as siblings or in-laws might be lifelong Big Bullies; alas, sometimes even spouses are. Coworkers and bosses—even people who consider themselves "friends"—might know just how to make you so afraid that you do whatever they say. You do not go after that promotion, or speak up at the staff meeting, for fear of what they might do to you. Sometimes, there is *nothing* these people can actually do to you, but in the moment it doesn't matter. The fear is so strong that you lose all sense of reason.

This Personality Type is called a *Big* Bully, because sometimes people try to be intimidating, and instead are simply pathetic. You can look them in the eye and throw it right back at them. Such a person is a sort of "bully lite," or "bully wannabe." If anything, these people help you feel *good* about yourself, because they make it seem like life is a cinch. But those who make you feel like life is instead a sub-stance often associated with walking a dog are *Big* Bullies. You obsess about them, and they make you feel too inhib-ited to do your very best.

HOW TO SPOT A BIG BULLY

Spotting bullies at the schoolyard is easy. Juvenile Big Bullies often *want* you to know this about them right off. But adults are not "supposed" to be this way, and so Big Bullies learn to be subtle. They might frighten you when no one else is around—or, if other people are present, they might say or do things that "between the lines" have a special meaning for you. The other people might not get what bothers you so much, and after being treated like you belong on perma-nent display at the National Archive of Paranoia, you decide to keep your fear to yourself.

So let's say you're new at the office. How can you tell if someone might be a Big Bully? One thing to look for is how much someone connects with you upon first meeting. If he or she seems distracted, unable to make eye contact with you, or does not draw you into the conversation, there is a fairly good chance this person will prove to be a Big Bully. That is to say, someone with no interest in relating to you as an equal, no empathy for how they make you feel, and who will use you to make themselves look superior to get ahead. If another coworker offers to take you to lunch with the gang, the Big Bully is likely to either not join in or else insist on taking over—choosing the restaurant, and so forth, even if it was not his or her idea in the first place. In these small but telling ways, the Big Bully is letting you know that you will not be able to have an equal say, or in any way predict what he or she will say or do next. At staff meetings or other conversations, this person will probably continue to avoid or ignore you as much as possible. If you make a good point or tell a funny joke, the Big Bully will not share in the enthusiasm, and instead will try to change the subject. In fact, speaking of subjects, their favorite one tends to be the face they see in the mirror, and they often have trouble talking about anything else.

Then comes the Big Moment. After not saying much of anything to you, the Big Bully will let you know that you have done something wrong. Whatever you have done right will not matter. The words will *not* go something like: "I know you've been working hard, but . . ." All that matters is this mistake you have made—whether you actually did it, or whether it even really *is* a mistake. In fact, your alleged offense was perhaps not even anything specific. Instead, you have hurt the Big Bully's feelings, or allegedly made him or her look bad, or "embarrassed yourself" without even realizing it. Probably, it is all so unexpected, and seems so out of proportion, that in the moment you freeze up. You have no idea what to do or say, and feel so bent out of shape, that the Big Bully has you just where he or she wants you. For if life can suddenly seem so unpredictably *bad*, you indeed have reason to be fearful.

A similar scenario can unfold in a family situation, or between so-called friends in a leisure activity. Whatever the specifics, the Big Bully is ready to prey upon the vulnerable—the new person at work, the new member of the family or club. Sometimes other people get along with the Big Bully perfectly fine—but often, another important clue is how others relate to him or her. If a fair number of people seem to avoid or argue with this person, or confide that they do not like him or her, that tells you something. And if you think that somehow you will be the exception—that the Big Bully will pick on other people but not you—then maybe you also believe that the Golden Gate Bridge is located in the Sahara Desert.

HOW DID BIG BULLIES GET THAT WAY?

Upon reading this question, you might be thinking: "Like I care." And you're right, why *should* you care about someone who treats you so meanly? But while it does not solve everything, getting a bit of perspective on these people can sometimes lighten your burden. So here it is:

Underneath it all, Big Bullies suffer from a poor self-image. That's why they pick on other people—to make themselves look better. They are easily threatened, and actually are quite frightened themselves—frightened of looking bad, of not impressing people, and of thereby being ignored. Sure, everyone wants to be popular, or get promotions at work. But for these people, it is more like this *must* happen. If they come across as an equal or too nice a person, they worry that someone else will then step all over *them*. In fact, on the inside they *do* feel stepped on all the time, in crazy ways that they never tell anyone else about.

It is extremely difficult to feel sorry for Big Bullies when they are picking on you. Nor should you feel that you have to—you have a big enough job taking care of yourself. But nonetheless, it can be useful to remember that they cannot be happy people. In the larger scheme of things, even when they seem to "win," they actually lose, because they have made more people distrust or even hate them. After awhile, if too many people do not like them and not enough people *do* like them, their worst fear might come true—they end up alone, with nothing.

Early in life, these people probably had reason to feel inferior. Maybe they came from a "poor" family, or one that was very unstable. Even within the family, someone might well have picked on them. But many people come from less than ideal backgrounds. If having a crummy family or getting picked on was enough to make you a bully, *everyone* would be a bully. When you get right down to it, Big Bullies are the way they are because other people let them get away with it. Their families tolerate the behavior, and maybe even defend it. Sometimes parents even let *themselves* get bullied around. School and other formative experiences likewise do not exactly bend over backward to change these habits. And the ironic thing about it is . . . it seems to work! The Big Bullies of this world often *do* get their own way. Even if eventually they lose it all (as was said not a moment ago), along the way they get a great many proofs that intimidating people and getting them to do what you want *will* give you more respect and power.

So besides trying to remember that these people are actually lonely and unhappy, you might also want to keep in mind that you are probably not their first target. You merely happen to be the next person they are encountering, and so it actually is nothing personal against you. In fact, if a Big

Bully sees you as a threat, on some level consider it a compliment. Just think—an extremely shrewd, manipulative person believes you are someone with real power. They think you are someone who could bully *them*.

HOW TO AVOID BIG BULLIES

As a child, you of course had little if any control over much of anything. You had no say when dinner was liver and Brussels sprouts, and you certainly had no control over where you went to school, or with whom. If a sibling bullied you and got away with it, then clearly your parents or guardians were not much help, either.

As an adult, you likewise do not have absolute say-so over every little thing that happens to you. Still, if you would truly rather live a life with *minimal* dealings with Big Bullies, you first of all might consider a career that is relatively low pressure and noncompetitive. You are probably *more* likely to encounter Big Bullies working in government or entertainment sectors, law or financial firms, or any company that talks a lot about how you can move your way up the ladder. It also never hurts to find out what the turnover rate is. If people seem to quit more than stay, what does that say to you?

While there are no absolute guarantees, jobs that tend to feature more team effort—such as think tanks, or technical or manual labor on a group level—might be less inclined to tolerate much Big Bullying. Often, teaching careers enable you to work fairly independently, and tenure can give you a bottom- line sense of security. Likewise, unionized positions offer many levels of protection. Also, if you are self-employed, or care more about feeling good than necessarily making a lot of money, you again might encounter fewer Big Bullies.

As for your personal life—if you are friends or partnered with a Big Bully, you probably have some deeper issues to work on, and in all seriousness should consider professional help. There are plenty of nice people to meet, and you deserve better than you are giving yourself. If the Big Bully is some sort of unavoidable relative like a parent, sibling, or in-law, you can still try to keep your encounters to a minimum. While it's always best to tell the truth, you might well be able to legitimately bow out of certain events. You also need not go out of your way to invite a Big Bully relative over, or call or e-mail this person.

When you *do* see a Big Bully relative, try to keep it within a group setting. Sometimes—not always, but *sometimes*—these people are less inclined to act out around other people. And if a Big Bully does start picking on you, a group setting makes it easier for you to disengage from the situation. You can say, "Sorry, but I just remembered I have to talk to So-and-So," and walk away. Do not be afraid to use the tried and true Blind Date Strategy—have a friend call you with an "emergency" at a certain time.

HOW TO BE AN ANTI-BULLY

While avoidance is sometimes possible, in other situations you might decide that the time has come to confront your Big Bully head-on. Maybe you yourself want to get ahead in this world, or simply are tired of being pushed around. So here are some tips for how to expose that Big Bully for the bratty coward he or she really is.

The worst thing you can do is come across as if the Big Bully is getting to you. Even if what you say is technically more clever or threatening, if you seem scared, nervous, on the verge of tears, or even angry, the Big Bully will know that he or she has won. So keep it super-cool. Think Clint Eastwood. (Or Clint*essa* Eastwood, as needed.) In other words, you can handle this person with one hand tied behind your back—maybe even with a yawn. You are not even close to breaking out in a sweat, and can barely even be bothered with him or her. Keep this general idea in mind, whether dealing with a casual acquaintance, someone at work, or a relative.

In Casual Encounters

If someone is acting like a total Big Bully jerk at a party or some such, you could just walk away, but at the same time you might have nothing to lose by letting 'em have it. When Big Bullies are going on and on about themselves, making some snide remark at you, or saying things that intentionally make them look good and you look bad, you can yawn and saying something like, "I'm sorry, I was thinking about something important. Did you just say something?" Say this as "innocently" as possible, as if the last thing on your mind is wanting to offend someone. If the Big Bully then says something to get back at you, respond with words to the effect of: "Oh gee, I'm sorry I hurt your feelings. I didn't realize you were *so* sensitive. Are you having a bad day? If you'd like, I can let other people know that they should go easy on you." What this type of thing does is communicate to the Big Bully that you are someone who brings all their insecurities right to the foreground, which is the last thing they want. So their instincts might tell them that you are someone to stay away from.

If the Big Bully becomes outwardly threatening or aggressive, you can say in your most sarcastic voice: "Gee, like I'm really scared. It's like I'll probably have a heart attack from fear." It could very well be that the other people listening will laugh, whereby once again the Big Bully decides you are someone to stay away from because you make him look bad.

At Work

If your boss is a Big Bully, then you obviously must tread carefully. By all means look for a different job—if nothing else, the process will provide a psychological sense of relief. But even if you must remain where you are, there are a few things you can do. One approach is to seemingly play along—but with the attitude of a self-possessed winner. If the boss is throwing his or her weight around a bit too much, respond with a crisp military salute and enthusiastically say, "Yes, sir/ma'am!" Rather than letting yourself be the human pincushion for your boss's needling, hold your head high and transform yourself into the best damn soldier in the company. If you seem *overly* polite and *overly* trying to please, the boss just might become uncomfortable, and end up saying, "Please stop saluting me or calling me 'sir/ma'am.' It isn't necessary." You see, underneath it all, Big Bullies assume no one will ever like them, so if someone actually *does* give them the respect they lust after, they often don't know what to do with it. And so you can disarm them.

The boss might not know what to make of you, and when a Big Bully is unsure, their instincts often tell them to back off.

If you are extremely secure in your job—virtually no chance of layoff, and what you do would be hard to replace—you might consider "humorously" throwing it back in the boss's face. If the boss rudely shouts out your name, shout out "What?" right back. And when the boss is going on and on at you, "jokingly" say something along the lines of: "Boy—do this, do that, it never lets up around here."

Humor might only get you so far—if the boss is a true louse, he or she might try to destroy your sense of humor, because he or she will see that, too, as a threat. So if the boss says to you, "This is no laughing matter," you can respond by being overly effusive: "Oh, I am so sorry if you got that impression. Would you like me to apologize in front of the rest of the office?" Once again, the boss is likely to back down.

The main point here is that it is harder to hit a moving target. If your Big Bully boss cannot successfully predict what you will say or do next, he or she is more likely to decide to leave you alone.

With a Big Bully coworker, you can try a lot of the same things. You also should keep in mind that the other people you work with have eyes and ears. Specifically, if your boss is *not* a Big Bully, he or she might be very impressed by how you handle this person without letting the conflict escalate. So if you treat a Big Bully coworker with a gushing degree of respect, other people might be impressed by your superior people skills. You will come across as someone who takes the high road, and is more concerned with keeping things harmonious than winning some trivial argument. So if people sense you are "humoring" the Big Bully, it might just win you the respect of your coworkers. You will seem a superior person.

In Your Private Life

As already mentioned, you hopefully do not feel bullied by your intimate partner or someone who is supposedly a "friend." But if you cannot avoid a relative or some friend of a friend, there are several steps you might consider for getting them off your back.

As always, remember to play it cool, because that Big Bully sister-in-law or stepbrother simply is more stubborn than you are. But the strategy is different from when you're at your job. Unlike being at work, you don't want to be super-obedient with Big Bully relatives, because you don't get paid and the amount of "favors" they may ask of you can be never-ending. Also, since these are truly personal dynamics, you can injure your inner self when doing things that simply cost you too much of your soul.

But what you *can* do is try agreeing with the Big Bully—at least on the surface. One technique is to come across as so humble that you deserve sainthood. If that sister-in-law or stepbrother goes on about what a lousy cook or provider you are, you can say in your most sincere tone of voice, "You're so right. I often cry myself to sleep at night, wishing I could make more money (or make better food, or whatever). I love my family *so* much, and I yearn to give them the best." Even if no one else is present, the Big Bully might actually experience a rare moment of mortification, and (drum roll, please!) actually *apologize*. Boy, whoda thunk it?

Another tactic is to agree with just the right touch of sarcasm. You can say: "I know, you're absolutely right. Why do I even bother? Should I run away now, or should I write a note first?" If, for want of knowing what else to say, the Big Bully nervously answers the question, you can then reply, "Thank you, I always knew you cared."

Still another way of "agreeing" is to take the criticism absolutely literally. You can say, "You're right, I'm a terrible provider. In fact, I make so little money that your visit is bleeding me dry, so you should leave." Or maybe better still: "If you'd like to write me a check to cover expenses, I will gratefully accept it." If you *really* want to stick it to them, then the next time they come over you can have all the power turned off, and serve nothing but bread and water. Or, if they criticize your cooking: "I know the food I made must be horrible, so here, let me take away your plate." If you want to gross things up, you can add: "If you have to throw up, you know where the bathroom is."

From these examples, hopefully you get the idea: beat them at their own game. The thing to bear in mind is that you can't really get "fired" from your family. Or if you *do* come from a culture with some fairly strict family rules, it would probably take something much more serious than this to get people to disown you. Besides which, some family members might appreciate how you stood up for yourself, and that someone finally put this annoying person in his or her place. So you might actually *gain* in family esteem out of the whole thing.

→ Ironically, you might take comfort in knowing that you are not the only person to get bullied. According to the American Justice Department, 25 percent, or one out of four children, will be bullied before reaching adulthood. The percentages on adult bullying have yet to be documented, but you might hazard a guess that they are certainly not any lower.

→ While many people are able to put bullying in perspective, some youths have a tragic inability to do so: 87 percent of teenagers believe that seeking revenge against bullies is the primary reason for high school shootings, according to Bureau of Justice statistics.

→ Bullying appears to be an important cause of suicide among children and adults. Numbers are difficult to measure, since suicide victims do not always explain their motives. But as public awareness increases, bullying increasingly is considered in the psychological profile.

the big mouth

CHAPTER TWO: Big Mouths don't know when to shut up. Or more to the point, it would never *occur* to them to shut up. At their least horrific, they are unbearably obnoxious. At their worst, they can humiliate you or even get you in trouble without a second thought. There's nothing wrong with wanting to be communicative; in fact, the world could use many more good communicators. But Big Mouths *live* to talk. "I talk, therefore I am." They are so compulsive about it that they do not even seem to notice that no one can stand them.

In their milder forms, Big Mouths are people who simply are afraid of quiet. Maybe you've had the experience of riding in the car with a Big Mouth. You're enjoying the scenery as you turn up the volume on the radio to hear your favorite song. "I *love* this song," you not so subtly hint. Good luck getting to hear it, though—because sitting next to you in the car is a Big Mouth. This Big Mouth cannot imagine a universe devoid of the sound of his or her own voice. And so for the ten millionth time you hear about how there's a sale on cocktail coasters, or how when the Big Mouth was in the sixth grade there was a leaky goldfish bowl.

But in their more extreme form, Big Mouths can screw you over. Since they never stop talking, they only care that they are saying *something*, and not the specific content. They will blab secrets or be tactless or even make things up just to keep hearing the sound of their own voices. Sooner or later they will say something that insults or embarrasses you, is simply not true, or maybe even gets you in trouble. And so your boss says to you, "I didn't know you were looking for another job," or thinks you are refusing to do the report you were asked to do, when what you really said was that you were going to the restroom. All thanks to the office Big Mouth. Or at a family event, the resident Big Mouth will blurt out to your tennis-loving dad that only idiots play tennis, or upon meeting your sister-in-law will say, "Oh, so *you're* the one who got the nose job that didn't go right."

The Big Mouth then proceeds to bore everyone with a long-winded tale (fueled by plenty of hot air) about how he or she is planning on refinishing a coffee table or how it makes no sense to like dogs more than cats. Speaking just a shade too loud—so that no one can interject—and leading a laughter chorus of one at the end of an allegedly amusing anecdote, the Big Mouth certainly does stand out in a crowd. In so-called group discussions, the Big Mouth has this way of not letting anyone else take a turn at saying something. Even on those rare occasions when someone else beats him to the punch, the Big Mouth interrupts, or tries to take over if there is even the slightest pause in what the other person is saying. The staff meeting or discussion group ceases to be about the topic at hand, and instead becomes a contest between the Big Mouth and everyone else.

HOW TO SPOT A BIG MOUTH

Once you know people for a while, it's elementary to tell if they are Big Mouths. If they simply never shut up, they are. But since when is life that easy? The thing is, when you first meet them, Big Mouths have this way of hiding their light under a bushel, so to speak. And so what will seem at first to be a perfectly reasonable person will soon enough prove to be a horrifying Big Mouth. And by then it might be too late. You will have made friends, become steady dates, or maybe even tied the knot. You will have ignored the warnings of others and agreed to go bowling with that Big Mouth in-law, or made friends with a Big Mouth coworker and cannot think of a way to get out of it.

There are, however, some warning signs to watch for. Believe it or not, sometimes Big Mouths seem to be extremely quiet people when you first meet them. They say little that first encounter. But watch their body language. They are not still, but are busying themselves with the saltshaker or running their fingers along the living room curtains. And when they *do* talk, it is probably something off the subject or very different in tone from what everyone else has been saying.

In other instances, the Big Mouth is fairly vocal on first meeting—and in fact might even seem quite jovial and polite. You are thinking you made a wonderful new friend. But with hindsight, you realize that this person was a little *too* jovial, a little *too* eager to please you and make friends. This seemingly okay person was a Big Mouth ready to pounce—or more to the point, ready to start talking nonstop.

Still another clue is that when these people talk, they do not say very much about themselves. Oh, they might go on and on about how they are thinking of buying a new toaster or how their second cousin twice removed is from Milton, Ohio. But underneath it all there is rarely much actual content. How they actually feel about their lives remains more or less a mystery.

The thing is, in spite of all the talk-talk-talk, Big Mouths are shy people. It might seem utterly nutty that someone who talks so much can be shy, but talk can in fact be used to keep people from getting close to you—as Big Mouths demonstrate with such inimitable flair.

HOW DID BIG MOUTHS GET THAT WAY?

Like a canine pedigree, Big Mouths are often born from the loins of other Big Mouths. Someone grows up in a home in which they could never get in a word edgewise. Either one family member dominated the conversation, or else pretty much everyone talked all at once. Or maybe they felt like whenever they said something, a parent or sibling was on their case, telling them how wrong they were.

Thus, they develop tremendous anxiety about talking to other people. Everyday conversations seem like Olympic competitions that they must psych themselves into being ready for. They are afraid that if they do not dominate the conversation, they will not be able to say anything. Big Mouths also fear being misunderstood, and so try not to say anything that is too personal. And as their name suggests, Big Mouths will proceed to talk up a blue streak, in the hope that if no one else gets to speak, no one will question what they say. They also fear that if they do not blow their own horns, no one else will have anything good to say about them.

The early years of feeling left out have left their mark. And so Big Mouths live in a kind of "Before" and "After" universe in which they never want to be perceived as that shy, socially inept person again. On the inside, they feel the same lack of confidence they always did, but they develop a way to somehow show off against this, as if rebelling against their own inner demons. In a way, there is something admirable in their efforts to mingle despite all their inner turmoil. But what they do not seem to understand is just how much they turn people off.

When they lose friends, Big Mouths take it the wrong way. Rather than explore how they might come across differently, they simply move on to the next person, or the next group. And so the whole thing becomes a vicious cycle. They talk too much, and alienate people—which makes them want to talk too much.

HOW TO AVOID BIG MOUTHS

As you'll see, Big Mouths are fairly easy to put in their place. Still, if you'd rather not have to mess with them in the first place, try as much as possible to stick to people you already know who are not Big Mouths. In other words, avoid unfamiliar social situations. If you do go to a party in which you have no idea what to expect, larger events are safer than smaller ones. At a big party you can always move away from an irritating Big Mouth, whereas in a small group you might be stuck. The same would hold true for religious or political groups, or for that matter bird-watching societies or just about any kind of group setting—big means *less* contact with Big Mouths. Obviously, certain kinds of groups are more likely to attract this particular type of showoff. Theater groups or (by virtue of their very name) *discussion* groups are fairly likely to have a resident Big Mouth.

If you must work with a Big Mouth, you can socialize with this person as little as possible. Go to lunch with other people, and hang out with other people at office parties. If you must attend meetings with a Big Mouth, you might be able to arrive late, leave early, or excuse yourself when a Big Mouth is going at it. Maybe there is an agenda for the meeting, by which you can plan accordingly. If there is *no* getting out of the meeting without jeopardizing your own career (or if your boss is a Big Mouth), perhaps you can discreetly work on something else while Big Mouth is droning on.

In your personal life, you can likewise not date or be friends with a Big Mouth. If you are partnered with a Big

Mouth and in other ways think the relationship is worth holding on to (but you do not want to confront the Big Mouth aspect), then busy yourself in the kitchen when you have company over, and try to organize events in which this person will probably be forced to keep his or her mouth shut for a little while. These can include live performances, be it a play or a concert—at the movies, people are more likely to get away with whispering asides, while before something live it might be considered rude. (Of course, this is more the case when a concert does not feature loud rock music.) Also, guided tours work here, or even self-guided tours of churches or old libraries.

If you have a Big Mouth relative, once again you can try to keep your contact to a minimum. If you go out of your way to call up a Big Mouth or invite one over, you have no one to blame but yourself. If you must see this person, you can volunteer to work in the kitchen or pick someone up at the airport, or make a run to the store for more mustard in order to get away for a while. You can also try to set up group activities or games that might likewise distract the Big Mouth for a few blessed minutes.

HOW TO SHUT UP A BIG MOUTH

Maybe people tend to be fairly tolerant of Big Mouths, because it seems so hard to make them stop. Actually, this is not true. You can usually shut a Big Mouth up with just a few well-chosen words. You might be thinking that that sounds mean, but you needn't feel guilty. It might actually be good for the Big Mouth to be reminded that other people like to be heard once in awhile, too. As stated back in the Introduction, you cannot change another person, but in this instance it can be helpful to offer the Big Mouth some constructive criticism. Unlike the Big Bullies of the last chapter, Big Mouths probably mean no harm. They simply are annoying, and underneath it all they would like to have better social skills. You can try to be as gentle as possible, but if you do hurt their feelings a little, remember that they are not being considerate of others themselves.

Since you want to get across that you are hardly a fan of the Big Mouth's big mouth, you want to set a positive example by showing how much can be said in as few words as possible. So when in doubt, err on the side of short communications. Get the idea across that every little nuanced point in the universe does not have to be spelled out in the minutest detail. Sometimes, the general idea is enough. And the general idea in this instance is: SHUT UP. You might be thinking: Why not get right to the point then, and utter those two utterly sublime words? The problem is that simply saying "shut up" can make it seem that you are the one with the problem—that you are a rude person, or in a bad mood. And so the Big Mouth might ignore you, and out of confusion or embarrassment so does everyone else. So you need to express yourself more effectively—briefly, and without too much detail, but effectively.

In Casual Encounters

At parties or other social encounters in which you have nothing to lose by getting a casual acquaintance to shut his trap, you might decide to go for it—as opposed to excusing yourself and walking away. Do not go out of your way to be mean, however. Also, be clear about your own motives. Some people *are* life-of-the-party types who keep others spellbound with their anecdotes. If you simply are jealous of someone's superior social skills, all you will do is embarrass yourself by trying to make her stop.

But if someone is droning on forever and the vibe in the room is that clearly everyone wishes he or she would stop—or if you are the only other person, and you would like a chance to say something as well—try one of the following suggestions. In a nonhostile way, you can make the "T" sign for "time out" with your hands, gesturing that there is something you would like to say. If there is a pause and you can get in a word edgewise, try not to come across as if now you will try to win the talking contest. If others are gathered around, you can say: "I think Mary wanted to tell us something." This will get across that you are striving for an equal conversation amongst everyone. If you really want to say something, you can begin with: "I just want to say one thing as briefly as possible." This might be perceived as a hint to the Big Mouth that sometimes modesty goes a long way.

If the Big Mouth fails to take any of these hints and instead (like the Energizer Bunny) keeps going and going, you might decide enough already, and take stronger action. With a friendly smile (so that you do not cause tension in the room), you can try holding up a sign that says: "5-Minute Warning." If the Big Mouth doesn't get it, then after a minute scratch out the "5" and hold up a sign that says: "4-Minute Warning." Ideally, the Big Mouth will laugh *with* you and take the hint. If he or she takes it a bit too seriously, lighten things up and say: "I was just kidding, Bob. But I do think that someone else would like to talk about *their* week, too."

At Work

If a Big Mouth is talking too much at a staff meeting, raise your hand and try to get the Chair's attention. If the Chair is the person talking too much, again urgently raise your hand. If there is a chronic problem of a Chair dominating too much of a meeting, this should be formally addressed within the work environment. If the boss or owner is the one who talks too much, you can try to flatter him or her by saying: "All this is great, and I think we all have a lot of questions and thoughts about what you've said." Or maybe: "Whoa, slow down—you're making so many good points and we can only comprehend so much at once. Can we please chew on just this much for awhile?" If you know your boss pretty well, maybe you can risk meeting with him or her in private and saying something like: "Could I offer some friendly advice? In my opinion, sometimes you tell us too much at once, and you might find it more effective to narrow things down more."

If a boss or coworker is talking too much to you while you're trying to get your work done . . . tell them. In a polite way, you can say: "This is interesting, but unfortunately I'd better get back to what I was doing." If a coworker is dominating too much of the conversation at a social event, you can try some variations on the acquaintance strategy outlined above. If it's your boss who is boring everyone to tears at a party, you just might be stuck. Afterward, you and your coworkers can at least commiserate on the ordeal you just survived.

But the workplace can see a more destructive aspect of the Big Mouth. In a fit of compulsive talking, someone might let slip something he or she was told in confidence. A word of advice: Never confide in a Big Mouth. That might seem like really obvious common sense, but there you have it. If you have confided in a Big Mouth and he or she has spilled the beans—or more to the point, *when* he or she has spilled the beans—you should clarify and defend yourself if need be with your boss. You should also tell the Big Mouth something like this: "Obviously, you cannot be trusted, so I won't confide in you again." If the Big Mouth starts trying to have an encounter group, denying that she said anything and so on, simply repeat yourself *one time*, and then walk away. Do not get into it in too much detail—it is unlikely any good will come of it.

If a Big Mouth coworker has blabbed something that was heard third-hand—let alone made an exaggerated or fabricated claim—you might well have grounds for some kind of formal grievance. Even just threatening such an action might compel the Big Mouth to think twice next time about spreading rumors about you. It probably is in your best interests to create a "paper trail" that documents the falsity of what was said, whether in the form of an e-mail apology from the Big Mouth, or if need be a more formalized action. If the Big Mouth apologizes, don't be shy about asking him or her to do so in front of whomever they blabbed to, unless so doing would be inappropriate. But in any case, since Big Mouths desperately want people to like them, they will probably be quite uncomfortable with being at the center of a storm, and might just emerge as better people from the experience. Or failing that, at least they will stay off your back.

In Your Private Life

If you have an intimate partner or close friend who is a classic Big Mouth and you feel you cannot stand it anymore, you owe it to both yourself and the other person to try to work things out. A good start is to let them know how you feel: "You are very important to me, but sometimes I wish you wouldn't talk quite so much. I like things to be quiet sometimes, and I also like to feel like I can contribute as much to the conversations as you do." If possible, by all means consider talking to a counselor or therapist together—some will work with friends as well as couples.

When there is a Big Mouth relative or friend that you must have occasional contact with, try to frame your concerns within a flattering context. For example: "Maybe no one has told you this before, but you are a very interesting person who naturally commands a lot of attention. So you don't have to try quite so hard. In fact, people might find you even more interesting if you hold back a little, and create an air of mystery." Or maybe: "You obviously have a very easy time speaking up, and I admire that about you. Now I'd like to be able to speak up more myself. Would you help me by giving me more of a chance to talk?"

If this approach does not seem doable—for example, if the Big Mouth in question is an older person who seems pretty much set in his or her ways—you are probably back to the avoidance techniques outlined earlier. But if there is really no good reason for having to tolerate the Big Mouth, and you have tried in nice ways to communicate your feelings about this behavior, then you might try something a bit more pointed. If possible, pull the person aside and say something like: "Bob, do you realize you just talked for thirty minutes nonstop?" If *that* doesn't work, then try to give other people a chance when the Big Mouth pauses for air, as outlined. This will not be perceived as much of a hint to the Big Talker, but it will at least provide temporary respite. You can also try to make it all into a kind of ribbing humor: "Bob, I'm amazed you never became a lawyer, given how you love to talk." Or: "Bob, I can see why you became a lawyer, given how much you love to talk." You might also try: "Bob, you're a great guy. You talk too much, but you're a great guy." Hopefully, everyone—including Bob—will laugh.

If a friend is spreading gossip about you, you might want to reconsider calling this person your friend. When a relative says all kinds of personal or untrue things about you, calmly and succinctly let them know how you feel: "It really hurts my feelings to learn that you said this about me. So much for being able to trust family." But don't go into it too much. You don't want to give them more to gossip about. And if the Big Mouth denies it, things can go from bad to worse. So say just enough; make it clear that this is not up for discussion, that in fact the Big Mouth is the last person you want to talk to right now, and that is that.

The main point is that Big Mouths are often one of the easier types of difficult people to handle. They seldom mean serious harm, and are relatively likely to prove capable of turning over a new leaf, once it is pointed out that their behavior is at least bothersome and possibly wounding to others.

→ The average person is said to spend one-fifth of his or her life talking. So most of us are far from silent, and many of us are probably Big Mouths at least occasionally.

→ Compulsive talking is associated with a range of larger conditions. On the one hand, it can be a symptom of neurosis or depression. On the other hand, it can be a sign of giftedness. Of course, both unhappiness and giftedness can be seen within the same person.

→ Not only do people sometimes talk too much face-to-face, but some have started to call themselves "blogging addicts" or "e-addicts"—people unable to stop communicating online.

BIG MOUTHS

the brick wall

CHAPTER THREE: You know the old saying about how talking to someone is like talking to a brick wall? Boy, do you know it. As a matter of fact, there is someone in your life who simply seems incapable of hearing anything you have to say. If this person simply said, "I understand what you mean, but I still disagree with you," it would not be nearly so bad. After all, you are a reasonable person; you do not expect everyone to agree with you all the time. But when you try to explain something to this delightful someone, it is as if you never even said anything. There is simply no getting through.

The Brick Wall can reveal his or her opaque face in all kinds of settings. Maybe there's a bit of small talk, such as who won the Super Bowl last year. Or maybe at work some sort of decision needs to be made about something. Or in your personal life, there is something you want very much for someone else to understand. Good luck with any or all of the above. Because the Brick Wall will leave you wondering if maybe you only *imagined* that you inhabited a body and voice in the physical dimension.

The other day, I overheard a Brick Wall in action. A guy said, "John Wayne was a great war hero." Someone else said, "Actually, John Wayne never served in the armed forces. He was only a war hero in his movies." (This is true, by the way.) Then the first guy said, "Well, all I know is that he was a great war hero." As you can see, a Brick Wall is incapable of saying, "Gee, I didn't know that," or even, "Are you sure that's true?" The second speaker's correct information might as well have not been uttered for all the effect it had.

Essentially, a Brick Wall uses one of three techniques to drive other people nutty. The first was outlined in the above example about John Wayne. This might be called the "Well-All-I-Know-Is" strategy. You say something that points out that what they just said was not quite right, and the Brick Wall counters with: "Well, all I know is . . ." and then proceeds to simply repeat him- or herself.

A second strategy is to latch on to one thing you said, and respond only to this one thing. Maybe you just made three or four points, but Brick Walls act as if they only heard one. This method is often used in letters or e-mails, as well. You bring up several issues with your sister-in-law, your landlord, or your gas company, and most of them are conveniently ignored.

The third technique used by Brick Walls is to say nothing. And if you're not careful, you can end up saying something you sorely regret as you try and try in vain to get a response out of this person.

HOW TO SPOT A BRICK WALL

Like the aforementioned Big Bully, some people become Brick Walls when they are barely out of training pants. As children, Brick Walls get right to the point. You can spot them literally putting their hands over their ears, refusing to hear what you say. Over time, this charming habit might be abandoned like so many Barbie dolls or G. I. Joes, but happily for the rest of us some people never do outgrow it. Of course, adults are less inclined to act out their discomfort in so obvious a manner, and learn to cover their ears *from the inside*, so to speak.

Even before you are exposed to a Brick Wall's mule-like stubbornness, there are ways of sniffing them out. Let's say you're new at work, or on a blind date. Elementary as it sounds, pay attention to this person's interactions with *other* people. Does he have a way of abruptly hanging up his cell phone, while you dimly hear the other party in mid-sentence? Does she ask the waiter to explain the specials after the waiter has just explained them? Do his coworkers seem to handle him as if feeding a wildebeest in a zoo, keeping a safe distance and saying not-so-tactful things about him behind his back? Despite all her protests that she has friends or close relatives or maybe even is married, does she seem like a loner?

The thing is, you are not exactly the first person in the history of the universe who finds Brick Walls exasperating, and so other people learn, in their way, to keep a safe distance. Even if the Brick Wall technically is rich, powerful, or famous, up-close and personal they have a way of turning people way, way off. Only a masochist of epic dimensions finds pleasure in talking to a Brick Wall. What should be a ten second discussion can take *hours* as you spin in circles of futility. Brick Walls are *always* suffering disagreements with others, *always* complaining about how this or that person is giving them a hard time. After a (hopefully short) while, you should get the idea that either a) the entire world is somehow plotting against this person, or else b) the problem actually lies with Mr. or Ms. Brick Wall.

Once you deal directly with a Brick Wall, expect it to happen again—and again and again. You will feel completely invalidated by them, and yet the temptation will be to try again, because maybe *this* time you'll get through. But of course you do not. For in this hard-to-put-your-finger-on way, it's almost as if the Brick Wall knows perfectly well what is going on, that without ever admitting to it there is a contest of wills at stake. And it is a contest that he or she has no intention of losing.

HOW DID BRICK WALLS GET THAT WAY?

You might be thinking: "Okay, bring out the violins." But it is nonetheless true that underneath it all Brick Walls are extremely insecure people. Life is, of course, often extremely complicated, and seldom are there easy answers. But Brick Walls keep thinking that these easy answers are out there; in fact, they would like to believe that they have found these answers. All people are sometimes confused or overwhelmed, but many people find a way to deal with life's ambiguities. They find a way to live in the gray area, where new information is permitted, existing beliefs can be replaced by new ones, and contradictions can be tolerated in moderation. In this gray area, it is permissible to say things like: "I don't know," or "I was wrong." But Brick Walls inhabit a strictly black and white universe. Something either is right and true, or it is wrong and false, *period*. And coincidentally enough, what is right and true happens to be whatever they themselves say or believe.

Oftentimes, these people grow up in environments in which they are exposed to virtually *no* gray area. They do not have a parent, teacher, or anyone else who sets an example as a free and open-minded thinker. And so the child models his or her behavior on the Brick Walls they see around them. Appearances can be deceiving here. Closed-minded people come from *all* walks of life. A worldly, ultraliberal artist can be a Brick Wall just as easily as anyone else—underneath it all, he or she might be utterly unwilling to respect what other people have to say. And so one generation of Brick Walls doth begat the next. Maybe there were a host of other problems growing up, or maybe things were relatively calm. In either case, the grownups spiritually had their hands over their ears, and the offspring followed their cue. Like their elders, the children decided that the way to appear important or impressive was to never admit that they were wrong. They are threatened by having to look very far inside themselves, because they have no experience with living comfortably with ambiguity.

Of course, sometimes kids *hate* it when their parents—or school or church—act this way, and they rebel. But the Brick Wall kid does not question what they are presented with. Ironically, perhaps they feel relatively loved, secure, and successful, and so they see no reason to doubt anything. Or maybe their brains simply are not wired to embrace life's complexities.

Over time, there once again is a vicious cycle. Brick Walls do not know how to listen and be open-minded and change their minds, and so they continue to ignore others, remain closed-minded, and stick to their guns no matter what. And they can only be more desperately stubborn with each new encounter.

Other people are not able to make much of an impact. Either they give up on the Brick Wall and cut off all contact, or else keep it all to a minimum, humoring the Brick Wall as needed. Or they might keep gallantly trying to get through—which usually means picking a fight with the Brick Wall—which will probably result in little more than more ill will and feelings of frustration. Whatever the scenario, the upshot here is that the Brick Wall is extremely unlikely to decide there is reason to change. Whenever possible, Brick Walls will surround themselves with people who do not question their authority. They become control freaks whose first and foremost commitment is to never having to acknowledge what they do not care to acknowledge. Alas, the big bad world is a place in which sometimes these people can go quite far in life. They may make a great many enemies along the way, but they might also butter up a few people here and there by doing them favors and seeming much "nicer" than their reputation would indicate. Plus there are those who will claim to admire Brick Walls from afar for "sticking to their guns." Even if the Brick Wall's mighty empire consists only of a few people, it will be ruled over with an iron hand. So once again, there is little incentive to change.

HOW TO AVOID BRICK WALLS

Happy is he or she who can simply avoid Brick Walls. As far as difficult types of people are concerned, Brick Walls are arguably the most exasperating. By their very nature, Brick Walls make it all but impossible to get through to them, so if you can tap-dance around them like an agile Fred Astaire, your dance through life might likewise be a merrier one.

Since Brick Walls tend to be extremely opinionated, you might be more likely to find them in highly fervent—some would say fanatical—settings. Extreme religious or political groups are likely to have their fair share of Brick Walls—which just might be your cue to stay away. When people are *that* inflexible in their thinking, do not be so naïve (or full of yourself) as to think you can up and change their minds. By all means try if you must, but you should not be surprised if you fail.

Sometimes even fan clubs can attract these kinds of people. The hero being worshipped gets arrested for something creepy, and the Brick Walls rally to say the charges *cannot* be true, simply *are* not true. In actuality, these fanatical devotees do not really know the facts—and will even ignore them once they are made known, if they prove unflattering.

In general, where there is heated debate, there is likely to be a Brick Wall. The controversy can be a weighty world issue, but it can also be about whether to replace a hedge in your backyard. In fact, no matter how seemingly small the issue, if your opponent seems unable to even recognize that you might have a good point, you can figure that you are about to confront a Brick Wall. And you may just decide to give the whole thing a rest.

At casual social events, it should be easy enough to avoid Brick Walls. Since they are so wrapped up in their own selves, they probably will not register any sort of hurt feelings if you simply walk away from them. If from a safe distance you see two or more people in a heated exchange, it might well be because one or more of them are Brick Walls.

When your coworker or boss is a Brick Wall, you might want to keep your important work-related discussions to a minimum. This is harder to do with a boss, of course, but even then report what you have to, ask questions about what you must, but do not go out of your way to seek his or her opinion if you do not have to. You do not want to jeopardize your own position, but whenever possible present information in terms of being already well under control, or even a *fait accompli*—a done deal.

If you are friends with a Brick Wall, you probably already space out your encounters so that you can appreciate the other good qualities this person has to offer without having to be made too pissed off too often by instances of profound stubbornness. But if you have not yet figured this out, you might want to try it. Also, you might want to avoid talking about things that are bound to lead to nothing but frustration when the Brick Wall refuses to budge an inch. Should the Brick Wall be someone *so* un-movable that you cannot even inspire a spirit of compromise—or even recognition of your opinion—over what movie to go see, you might want to think twice about continuing to call this person a friend.

Being partnered to a Brick Wall can be extremely frustrating. Such a person is unlikely to even admit or acknowledge there is a problem, and so it will be quite difficult to talk things out, let alone seek professional help. But if you want to tough it out with this person—and also believe that it will do little good to confront him or her—you can try to work around this immovable object as often as possible. If the matter at hand need not involve joint counsel, simply take action by yourself. You can always inform your partner after the fact that you went ahead and bought groceries, paid the bills, made dinner reservations, or went for a walk with a friend. Once again, you might want to avoid what you know will be a difference of opinion, be it over politics, religion, or what the best show on TV is.

When Brick Wall relatives are in positions of power within the family, you might have to decide whether to grin and bear it or simply keep your contact to the barest possible minimum—or even risk being written off by this person, if you truly cannot stand it. Yet whatever the nature of your relationship to said relative, you again can try to avoid touchy subjects, or other matters that lend themselves to the lengthy expression of opinions. Busy yourself with other activities when you do get together, and do not go out of your way to seek this person's opinion.

HOW TO MAKE A BRICK WALL CRACK

It is *extremely* difficult to make any headway with Brick Walls. The angrier you get and the more you insult them, the more likely it is that they will stick to their guns. When they are extremely good at what they do, they will not even show a trace of emotion, or anything else (such as a body language cue) that indicates they have heard what you have said. Life is never all we want it to be, and you might well be best off resigning yourself to the harsh reality that there are some people you simply cannot get anywhere with.

Still, if you are determined to give it a try—if you feel you simply cannot live with yourself by letting go of whatever it is—you should proceed very, *very* cautiously. You should be mindful of the potential seriousness of the situation, as well as your own emotional condition: Are you likely to simply feel worse by confronting this person? Might your life become needlessly complicated if you do? For you need to remember that ultimately it is not really about you, but some deeper problem that the Brick Wall has—and that you are probably not the first person to have this kind of toxic reaction to him or her.

Even when confrontation with a Brick Wall does not escalate to the level of lawyers and court hearings, it might feel as though it is at that level. These are not friendly encounters, but are extremely defensive and hostile, with the potential for tempers erupting in damaging ways. Even if you have known the person all your life, you will feel as though it is the coldest of impersonal settings, because there will be little if any glimmer of any goodwill. The Brick Wall is willing to abandon any sort of warm fuzziness for what he or she believes is the much more important principle of not having to admit personal error. This should tell you something about how this person actually feels about you, should the lack of empathy come as a shock.

You might well be better off leaving the room if you feel you are about to lose your temper. Perhaps you can take out your frustration in closing the door just a bit too loudly behind you, but letting the other party know your general displeasure might be about as good as it is going to get. Splitting hairs over even more specifics is unlikely to get you anywhere, and if you completely lose your temper you might say or do something that makes you look bad, or needlessly complicates your life.

Another *extremely* important thing to remember is that victory over Brick Walls is a subtle thing. No way are they going to say outright, "I hear what you are saying and apologize for not recognizing it and from now on will do things differently." But what *might* happen is that their actions will speak louder than words. For example, if you want your Brick Wall neighbor to stop playing loud music, despite the blank reaction you get to bringing it up, perhaps the neighbor actually *will* lower the volume—at least some of the time, anyway.

Nonetheless, the best you might be able to hope for is a kind of spiritual victory. If other people are present they might bear witness to how reasonable you are being while the other person is not. Should other people not be present, or should the Brick Wall wield so much power to intimidate that others simply are afraid to speak up, then seek solace from within yourself. Think of it as a movie in which you are the star, and despite the plot developments, the audience can see that you are a hero.

Framing it in terms of an innocent question is *not* likely to do much good. If you seem utterly uncommitted to a given point of view or not even sure what to believe, the Brick Wall will simply think: "Why should I give in to this?"

So you need to seem committed to your stance. You need to be thorough, yet brief and to the point. You need to keep the focus on the specific matter yet also try to seem personable. And as if that were not enough of a balancing act, you must come across as having conviction of belief yet also as an open-minded person who (unlike the Brick Wall) is willing to listen to other points of view.

Brick Walls do not vary much across situations, given the way they retreat within themselves and therefore depersonalize you. But for what it is worth:

In Casual Encounters

At a party or similar social event, you probably have little to lose (albeit likewise little to gain) by simply telling someone he is being a jerk, and are not listening to anything you say. You could of course also just walk away from such a person; the choice is yours.

At Work

You need to know exactly what the facts are, have irrefutable proof of them, and proceed as methodically—and yet as simply—as possible. Do not let your frustration show; simply say, "You are not answering my question," with as little emotion as possible, when the Brick Wall tries to evade the issue. Outnumbering the Brick Wall is probably a good idea. A surprise attack also is probably a wise move.

When your boss is a Brick Wall, you probably need to build up a great deal of trust before confronting him or her—and even then you must be very careful not to take things too far. Express a different viewpoint, and then let it go if you get virtually no response.

In Your Private Life

A Brick Wall can make quite a powerful ally if he or she is on your side.

If the Brick is an old friend, a close relative, or a significant other—it might be possible to appeal to a deeper sense of loyalty. However seemingly indifferent Brick Walls behave, you might be able to remind them of some previously shared good experience you had together. Perhaps you can also say something like: "Remember when you corrected me when I thought we should do such-and-such? Now I'm glad you did, and I'd like to return the favor. This time around, it's my turn to be right [do not say the Brick Wall is wrong!] and help you to see that what you need to do is, etc." But once again, do not faint from shock if you make little if any headway.

➔ In Freudian terms, excessive stubbornness is associated with unresolved conflicts at the anal stage of development, along with excessive meanness, orderliness, and stinginess.

➔ Research suggests that women are more likely to accuse men of being Brick Walls—of never listening to them—than men are of accusing women of the same thing. Though, of course, sometimes the roles are reversed.

➔ In couples' therapy, showing no response to what your partner says is sometimes called "stonewalling." Being the victim of a spouse's stonewalling can result in an increased heart rate.

BRICK WALLS

the constant complainer

CHAPTER FOUR: Some people in this crazy world love one thing and one thing only—namely, *nothing*. They can never say anything good about anyone or anything at any time. While other passengers in the car admire the beautiful scenery, the Constant Complainer is ragging on about how it is too hot or too cold. If you turn the air conditioner on, it makes a noise that drives them crazy. If you open a window, Constant Complainers stress over how the wind is spoiling their hair. There is always a problem with the service in the restaurant, always something the matter with the food, always a major problem over leaving the tip.

The Constant Complainer's talents are quite versatile, and are not limited to trivia by any means. He or she is also most adept at telling you why you picked the wrong college, the wrong major, the wrong job, the wrong partner, the wrong friends, the wrong mortgage rate, the wrong name for your pet iguana, and so forth.

If you make the mistake of going to such a person for a little encouragement or moral support, forget it. When you say something like, "Maybe my boss will give me the raise I asked for," the Constant Complainer will be somehow incapable of replying, "Yeah, maybe you will—good luck." Instead, you will hear words to the effect of: "Are you kidding? Why would they give *you* a raise? They probably barely make ends meet." And if you *do* get the raise, the Constant Complainer will admonish you to be wary of your new higher tax bracket, or talk about how with prices going up you will never even notice the extra money. (For good measure, they also might throw in something about how wasteful you've always been, so the money will just slip through your fingers.)

In effect, their outlook toward others seems to be: "Don't bother." Are you thinking of repainting your living room? Don't bother, you'll only make it worse. Are you thinking of calling someone back to say you changed your mind? Don't bother, you will only confuse things.

Given how bad everything always is for these people, it is truly commendable that they are able to dispense advice so liberally. In essence, no one who travels even casually through their world does anything but create havoc and ruin. Even when others try to rectify things, all has degenerated way beyond the point of repair. Offering to make it up to the person, to pay them back, or see a therapist together to work out whatever it is will obviously only make things worse, and how dare you even make the suggestion?

Oddly enough, though these people seem to think that everything about the universe stinks, they often do not tolerate negativity in others. If *you* have had a bad day at work, or split up with your sweetheart, or your cat just died, the Constant Complainer is likely to say something like: "Oh, get over it. What have you got to complain about? That's just how life is." Or maybe: "Look, I just don't want to talk about this now." Presumably they have much more important things to do.

HOW TO SPOT A CONSTANT COMPLAINER

This is hardly a challenging task. Unlike some kinds of difficult people, Constant Complainers are very, very bad at hiding what they are like, even upon first meeting. In fact, they are often so swept up in their tornado of negativity, that it would not even occur to them to be any other way. The mistake you might make is to think that the person in question is simply "having a bad day," or some such. If someone is simply having a bad day, they are usually pretty good at keeping it to themselves. Seeming a little moody or sad is not the same thing as nonstop whining. Besides, even if you're meeting someone for the first time, a mutual friend might say something like: "Go easy on Betty today. She just broke up with her husband." In which case even a saint might be forgiven for being a bit out of sorts.

In casual social situations, there might well be a restaurant or living room blind that inspires the ire of a Constant Complainer. In a work setting, be on the lookout for people who never like *anything* about *any* of your ideas. On a blind date, see if whatever you bring up is met with a totally contrary response. If you mention that you think that people become vegetarians for such and such a reason, the Constant Complainer will reply that no, it is for some other reason. When you say that you're thinking about getting a new job, the reply might well be an utterly incredulous *"Why?"* as if to suggest that only the most hopelessly demented of persons would consider such a thing.

In fact, whatever you want to do, there will be some reason why you should not do it. If you say, "I think I'll take my vacation in July," or for that matter, "I think I'll take out the garbage," the Constant Complainer will be right there to counter-argue why you should not. July will be a *terrible* time of year to vacation, and it will make no sense whatsoever to take out the garbage. These people are not beyond critically questioning even your desire to get a glass of water or use the bathroom.

Another giveaway is the state of their physical health. Ailments that baffle the medical profession inhabit Constant Complainers with alarming frequency. Aches, pains, itches, and ouches that doubtless signal the presence of yet undiscovered fatal illnesses are but one of the many burdens they must shoulder through each agonizing moment of existence. If someone you just met is going on and on about the agonizing pain they are in, and you ask them if they've been to the doctor, be mindful of replies such as:

"My doctor doesn't know anything," or: "My health insurance is run by a bunch of crooks. You think they would actually let me see a doctor?"

Moreover, while everyone likes some people more than others, the Constant Complainer has nothing but bad things to say about pretty much everyone. That they even bother to stay in touch with other people when they are so beleaguered should qualify them for the Nobel Peace Prize. (But of course, the whole thing is rigged anyway, so they will never get what is their due.)

Even extremely trivial matters such as someone else beating them to a parking place can launch a litany of belly-aching. Not that they are likely to say as much to the offend-er. Instead, Constant Complainers like to keep things to themselves—which translates into dumping it all onto the nearest available ear. But they seldom actually confront the people who get on their nerves. This is another way to spot them. If you say to such a person, "Have you tried talking to your mother about this?" or "Why don't you write a letter of complaint to the electric company?" there will probably be some reason for why such is not possible. You see, the thing is while everyone needs to vent now and then, Constant Complainers actually *like* to complain, and would not know what else to do with their time.

HOW DID CONSTANT COMPLAINERS GET THAT WAY?

Constant Complainers often come from one of two kinds of families. Sometimes they grow up in a household of other Constant Complainers, and so as they grow older all they know is to complain. Maybe they told themselves when they were younger that they would never turn out the same way—and maybe they even have convinced themselves that since they complain only twenty-three hours a day instead of twenty-four like their parents did, they are not complaining people at all. But the truth is, they absorbed far too much of this behavior to shake it loose. What other people perceive to be annoying and negative these people take to be "normal."

Another way Constant Complainers come into being is if they grow up in households that are at the opposite extreme. They were never allowed to complain about *anything* as children. Perhaps their parents were "religious" in an unhealthy way, or simply neurotic about hearing any bad news. And so they felt utterly censored. What seemed to them to be very real problems were treated as if they did not exist. And so, once on their own, they feel a need to express all that pent-up frustration. Anyone who does not see things in the same negative way as they do are considered "the enemy," which is to say stand-ins for their families.

But whether they think they are being "normal," or are acting out against their families, Constant Complainers feel very misunderstood. And they deeply resent feeling this way, because from their point of view what they are saying is correct, and it is everyone else's problem for not agreeing with them.

HOW TO AVOID CONSTANT COMPLAINERS

Constant Complainers might be more likely to be encountered in group settings in which the *purpose* is to complain.

Sometimes these groups have very idealistic intentions. They might be aimed at changing public policy in a more humane direction, and by all means you should want to join in such endeavors. But just be aware that some people join these political, humanitarian, or religious groups because they truly believe in the cause, others join them as an extension of their essentially negative view of life. In asserting that such and such a policy should change, they are *really* saying: "I hate everything and everyone." Be prepared for a laundry list of complaints that go way beyond the issue at stake.

The same holds true for self-improvement groups. Some people engage in group therapy out of a genuine desire to improve. But others see it simply as another venue for complaining . . . and complaining and complaining. They might even go so far as to try to hold you back from making progress, because if you let go of whatever is bothering you, you will become "one of them." This person will be sort of like a whiny Peter Pan who takes you not to Neverland but to a garbage dump, yet still tries to stop you from growing up.

If you encounter a Constant Complainer at a party or on a blind date, it ought to be easy enough to make your excuses and depart from his or her company. Constant Complainers expect everything to go lousily, anyway, so you might actually be *pleasing* them by cutting things short.

At a job, you can try to ignore Constant Complainers as much as possible by not socializing with them. Even if you must work side by side with one, you can make sure you spend your lunch hour in different company. Constant Complainers will more than likely find someone else to dump on, so again, there is no need to feel guilty.

If you are partnered with a Constant Complainer, once again you should consider professional guidance for either or both of you. This person has deep issues that need sorting out, and your level of intimacy will be hampered unless this happens. If a relative is a Constant Complainer, then set yourself up in situations that keep your contact to a minimum. Besides doing the obvious (not going out of your way to call her, and so forth), you can try arranging situations in which her complaining is kept as far away from you as possible. For example, maybe you and other family members can chip in to send this person to a health spa or on an ocean liner cruise. In this way, it will be obvious that you have not neglected this person by virtue of your generous gift. And if she in fact hates the Caribbean cruise or the Swedish massage, at least you will not have to hear about it directly.

If you want Constant Complainers completely out of your life, you can write them a letter—face to face they are likely to guilt-trip you. Make it plain and to the point that you simply do not want their negative influence in your life anymore.

HOW TO HAVE NOTHING TO COMPLAIN ABOUT

If you *must* work with, live with, or visit with Constant Complainers on a regular basis, there are things you can do that might keep their annoying droning to a minimum—at least when in your own company.

One of the *least* productive things you can do is to counter their negativity by saying something positive. More than likely, the Constant Complainers will rebel against this, and try to counter with something even more negative.

And besides, you supposedly do not want to totally alienate them, for whatever reason.

Instead, you might try beating them at their own game. Agree with them, and then some. Do *not* let this take the form of joining in with your own negativity. That will turn into fire feeding fire. The Constant Complainers will feel dangerously close to you, and you will feel uncomfortable and exhausted. So keep the focus on the Constant Complainers. Agree so very much that they start to undo themselves.

In Casual Encounters

If you feel you must stay engaged in conversation with a Constant Complainer at a social event—let's say it's your boss's spouse, or you are trying to impress your date by showing how socially engaging you are—then you probably do not have much to lose by simply listening, nodding, and smiling in affirmation. After a discreet interval, you can shake hands and say how nice it was to meet this person. If you're stuck riding on a bus or airplane with a Constant Complainer you never met before—and this slight detail will hardly stop them from dumping on you—you can likewise give the appearance of agreeing, letting your mind wander. If it is a long trip, you can probably pretend to fall asleep, or after awhile say that you have to work on your laptop, or listen to a CD for work.

At Work

A coworker who constantly complains can be a highly destructive influence in your life. For one thing, such a person can drag you down into the muck and mire of their bad attitude. Also, if you become too closely associated with a Constant Complainer, other people will start to assume you have the same bad attitude, and this can socially ostracize you. You might be bypassed for promotions, or even just kept out of the general loop.

If the Constant Complainer has been working there for some time, study the behavior of other veteran employees. If the Constant Complainer is new at the job, keep a safe distance.

If you must work closely with this person, you can first of all sort out in your mind what is work-related from what is not. When it comes to topics that are not related to work, you can try saying something like: "Your mother-in-law sounds like a very difficult person, but I'm worried we might not finish this report in time. Maybe we can talk more about your family some other time." And then you can make a point to not be socially available.

If the Constant Complainer persists, you might try saying, "I'm sorry—I make it a point not to get involved in the personal lives of the people I work with. It's nothing personal against you, I'm the same way with everyone."

As for complaining *about* work, you can respond as follows: "Wow, you sound really unhappy here. I think you should strongly consider looking for a different job." If the Constant Complainer has some list of excuses for why that is not possible, you can say: "I guess you really are trapped, then." The Constant Complainer might then be caught off guard, and deny that such is the case, or that the job is really as bad as all that.

If your boss is a Constant Complainer, you might want to look for another job, so that you can be in a more positive work environment. If you think that you are in an advantageous position by being your boss's trusted confidant, you might want to think again. Still, you are better off listening to your boss than trying to minister positive vibrations. Not only will your boss rebel like any other Constant Complainer, but he or she might also try to take advantage of you if you act too much like some sort of overly helpful nurse. Next thing you know, the boss will be dumping *everything* on you. So if your boss is going on about his or her personal woes, just say, "Gee, that sounds really bad," and then slip in some totally work-related question that changes the subject. If your boss is complaining a lot about the work environment, you might want to innocently ask: "Have you done anything to change this?" The boss might well feel trapped, because he is on the verge of exposing his own limited power or shortsightedness insofar as handling this situation. After being asked a few times why he did not use his position of power to greater advantage, the boss might just cool it with you—though do not be surprised if he then complains to others that you are a "bad listener."

In Your Private Life

As earlier stated, you owe it to yourself and your partner to consider professional counseling if you are mated with a Constant Complainer. If this is not possible for some reason, and you do not want to end the relationship, you can once again opt for a strategy of agreement. When the Constant Complainer is going on about her lousy childhood or job or whatever and finally pauses for a gulp of air, you can interject: "Gee, that's interesting. I never thought of it that way before." If you know from bitter experience that if you try out ideas on this person you will be met with a big loud "no," then keep your ideas more to yourself. Take action, instead. If there is always a disagreement when you say you are going to take out the garbage, then just go take it out without announcing that you are about to do so. Do as many small things as possible without running them by your partner first.

Now, if it is something major—like looking for another job, or what to do about one of your kids—you will have to talk it out first. When your partner does his or her very pre-dictable thing of thinking all your ideas are wrong or bad, honesty might well be the best policy: Tell him or her how you feel. You might say: "I'm feeling very frustrated, because I want us to find a way of dealing with this, yet all I'm hear-ing is that my ideas are bad." Keep the emphasis on how *you* feel, without being accusatory. You can also try asking your partner what his or her ideas are. If your partner does not have any ideas, you should feel free to say something along the lines of: "In that case, I guess we're stuck with my idea." If your partner does have ideas and they are good ones, then everyone wins. If you genuinely believe your partner's sug-gestions are bad, you might want to say: "I guess the tables are turned, because just as you didn't like my ideas, now I don't like yours. Let's see if we can meet in the middle."

If you have a friend who is a Constant Complainer and you want to preserve the friendship, listen, briefly agree that her life is indeed beyond misery, and try to change the subject. If you yourself are down in the dumps, try to con-fide in someone else, because the Constant Complainer will probably just drag you down further. Plus the topic of conversation will probably shift away from you to them, and you will end up having to once again listen to the same old thing. So for what it's worth, you won't even feel comforted.

If you have Constant Complainers for relatives whose company you must endure, utterly agree with them and take their side. In fact, take it so far that they end up backing away. For example, if your stepfather or younger sister is going on endlessly about their lousy job or mysterious health ailment or impossible ex-, you can say: "I am just in awe of how you withstand such torture. Let me call the local newspaper—they should do a feature on you."

In other words, you make it apparent that if Constant Complainers think you will be a mere passive ear, they have another thing coming. Probably after awhile, the Constant Complainer will learn to cool it when you are around.

→ Research done by the Mayo Clinic among other sources has suggested that optimists live longer on average than pessimists—that a pessimistic outlook might be associated with less resistance to various kinds of ailments. (So maybe there is some validity to the Constant Complainer's health problems.)

→ What is termed "defensive pessimism" can be psychologically useful. It means that you work through the worst possible scenarios in advance of a situation, in order to prepare for it. (Of course, this does not mean you have to share these horrific visions with others.)

→ Are you a closet Constant Complainer? Some research suggests that people who complain all the time and the people they complain to tend to share the same attitudes.

CONSTANT
COMPLAINERS

the drama queen

CHAPTER FIVE: You could say that the Drama Queen is kissin' cousin to the Constant Complainer. Both types of difficult people will go on and on about how wretchedly miserable everything is. But while the Constant Complainer simply gets off on being hyper-negative, the Drama Queen's alleged crises are meant to signal that the Drama Queen is a star. Drama Queen types want constant attention and pampering from other people, and so their problems must become *everyone's* problems. They think that if you try to fix things for them, it means you love them. Or, if you cannot fix things, you can at least have them foremost in your mind—which of course takes a lot of reminders, courtesy of the Drama Queen. If something had an easy solution, there would be no drama—and hence, no star. So basically, everything is constantly unfixable, even while the Drama Queen craves your help and interest.

For Drama Queens, life is an endless mess. There are always a million different people who are being mean to them, or preventing them from doing something, or suing them, or are being sued *by* them, or whatnot. Soap opera characters have nothing on Drama Queens. When their houses are not burning down, they are getting ripped off by their accountants, disowned by their grandmothers, and who knows what else. Tragedies do, of course, visit everyone from time to time. And perhaps on occasion you have said or done something that you later regretted, because it made your life needlessly complicated. But Drama Queens live in the major crisis mode 24/7. So many bad things happen to them all the time, that after awhile you cannot help concluding that they do it to themselves. In a normal day, they are on the phone for *hours*, threatening this person, seeking solace from the next one. If they can afford it, they might keep an attorney on retainer, so that they are ready to pounce at any moment. In a way, though, less affluent or powerful Drama Queens are even more melodramatic, because they can depict themselves as even more the helpless victim.

For Drama Queens, there is always a complicated hodgepodge of reasons for why whatever it is cannot be resolved. They cannot change their diets or go on or off medication because something else will go wrong if they do. They cannot change their job, because there is a clause in their mortgage that says something or another. While other people are able to organize and compartmentalize their lives, with Drama Queens everything spills over into everything else. They also have an extremely difficult time being alone. A single evening with no place to go or no one to talk to can be experienced as an emergency of such epic proportions that World War Three would seem trivial by comparison. You must help the Drama Queen, and you must help him or her *now*.

HOW TO SPOT A DRAMA QUEEN

When you first meet a Drama Queen, you probably will decide that he or she is an exceptionally charismatic person. The Drama Queen is normally a highly skillful storyteller, capable of holding an audience's attention with one funny, outrageous tale after another. Quite often, the Drama Queen has cultivated a distinct way of laughing, and peals of his or her own laughter will roar above the merriment of the crowd at the conclusion of an anecdote or joke. Even in more serious or businesslike settings, Drama Queens will tend to dominate the conversation. If they must listen to someone else, they will still somehow pose or position themselves in a way that makes them stand out from the crowd. In theatrical terms, they are scene-stealers.

At first, you might well be in awe of this person, and feel honored that they have singled you out for attention. It is as if you have been sprinkled by stardust. These people often create a chummy sense of conspiracy, as if it is the two of you against the world, and together you notice absurd things that other people do not. You might well decide that this is the most marvelous, magical person you have ever met.

However, nagging little doubts will start to creep in early on. In fact, you might start finding that when you see this person face to face you are as dazzled as ever, yet when you think about him or her afterward you are angry, and you may not even be sure why. Maybe it has to do with the way you must always defer to the Drama Queen; there is only one star in *this* movie, thank you very much. Even if you are supposedly developing an intimate relationship, you feel more like the person's personal assistant—or maybe even her disciple. Yet whatever the nature of the relationship, it does not feel democratic. It is more like a benevolent dictatorship. If you will be what the Drama Queen wants you to be, he or she will be generous with the crumbs thrown your way.

There will reach a point of crisis. Quite often in the middle of the night, or while you are at work or have made other plans well known to the Drama Queen, you will get an "urgent" phone call. The sky is falling. The world is ending. The Drama Queen has a hangnail. You will be expected to drop whatever you are doing and rush to his or her aid.

After awhile, you start to learn that there are all kinds of problems the Drama Queen is juggling around at the same time. This louse is getting the Drama Queen fired, while this other SOB has complained about the Drama Queen's pet ferret. And while case by case these seem like things that can happen to anyone, the fact that there are so many problems all the time make you wonder if this person really is worth knowing.

Once you let the Drama Queen down—once you do not show up when summoned, or fail to help or worship him adequately—you will either be yelled at or else summarily dropped. In the case of the former, run for the hills, mildly scolding yourself for not heeding all the warning signals. If the latter is the case, count your blessings and move on.

Not all Drama Queens are alcoholics or drug addicts, and not all drug addicts and alcoholics are Drama Queens. Still, there is a tendency for someone with serious drug or alcohol issues to take on this type of difficult personality.

HOW DID DRAMA QUEENS GET THAT WAY?

As children, Drama Queens never feel like normal kids. Sometimes they grow up spoiled and overly pampered; they are very much the apple of Mommy or Daddy's eye, and everything they say or do is wonderful and perfect. They might be an only child, or perhaps have a sibling or two that compare negatively to the Drama Queen, who is smarter or more talented by comparison. The point is especially punctuated if there is *one* other child, whereby the sibling rivalry seems unequivocally won by the Drama Queen.

Sometimes these parents inflate not only the child's ego but also his or her achievements. Honorable mention in a spelling bee becomes first place upon retelling. These children grow up feeling "special," but there is a price tag attached—it means that they must *always* be special, or else they will not get the kind of pampering and attention they think is love. And stretching the truth—not to mention outright lying—comes to be seen as perfectly normal.

Flipping the coin over, Drama Queens can also emerge from childhoods in which they felt ignored. Perhaps they came from a family with a large number of children, and so there was only so much attention to go around. Or maybe some other child in the family was favored. Or maybe the parent who *did* favor the Drama Queen dies or moves away.

In any case, the Drama Queen felt as if he or she deserved more attention than was given. Maybe this child *was* a good speller—or athlete or singer—and yet the family acted as if it could have cared less.

While most everyone likes movies, for the fledgling Drama Queens movies become like a Holy Grail. Probably there are a few films or movie stars in particular that the Drama Queens choose to emulate. Because only then do they feel the kind of glamour or excitement that they believe to be their due. From there, it is but a small leap toward infusing their lives with a similarly heightened sense of drama. If Hollywood is not knocking, they will make do with Tallahassee, or whatever town they live in.

Drama Queens' lives gravitate toward extremes, so it is not surprising that they feel either like outcasts in school, or else are voted Most Popular. Or sometimes, it oddly can be a bit of both: mocked or misunderstood by some, yet admired and emulated by others. But whatever the specifics, they do not feel a natural sense of blending in. Bonding with others is an ongoing campaign; it takes *work*. No matter how intensely they sometimes seem to bond with others, a part of them is always on the outside looking in.

Somehow, whatever they do achieve, it is never enough. Even if they become *actual* Hollywood stars, they need more, more, more. In fact, sometimes success serves only to raise the ante. In order to feel *special*, they cannot feel run-of-the-mill, and so yesterday's success may not mean very much today.

Somewhere along the way—often with the onset of puberty—their intense desire to win favor takes on all sorts of complications. Their childish ways of fibbing take on greater significance when dating and budding sexuality are involved. Normal adolescent rebellion gets mixed up with their deep need to always stand out from the crowd. If their zealousness is not kept in check, they might end up starring in *Hello, Dolly!* as performed by the San Quentin Players.

A lifetime of bad habits come into being as the Drama Queen becomes entangled in all sorts of messes. (And if substance abuse is involved, it becomes all the more difficult to keep track of it all.) Since the Drama Queen has little if any sense of perspective, it can all seem much more important than it is. And since they do not think of anyone but themselves, Drama Queens might simultaneously *minimize* in their minds the harm they are causing others. Stars of such magnitude, of course, are not held to the same standards as the rest of humanity—and moreover, they should not have to get their fingers dirty. And so it becomes essential to their self-image that they find other people to listen to their troubles, and try to fix it all. Or that is to say, fix it all for about thirty seconds, until some new crisis erupts.

HOW TO AVOID DRAMA QUEENS

Obvious as it sounds, anything pertaining to showbiz (and that includes amateur groups) is likely to have its fair share of Drama Queens. Actors, singers, and musicians of all varieties are not unknown to be Drama Queens. Creative people in general (such as artists or writers) can also be this way, as can politicians, athletes, or people who start their own businesses—or for that matter, even criminals. In so many words, anyone who does something that relatively few people do, and which has either brought them attention or could potentially bring them attention, might indeed prove to be a Drama Queen. If you go to work for such a person, or for a company that deals with any of these kinds of people, don't say you weren't warned. Of course, not all people with exceptional careers are Drama Queens; it's just that finding one among them is not exactly the strangest thing that ever happened.

Even in other fields, someone can be, say, the star lawyer of their firm, the star doctor at their hospital, or even the Number One salesperson for their company. And while once again, this does not automatically mean that such a person is a Drama Queen, be mindful of the way he or she behaves. In school environments, teachers or professors who seem to welcome being "worshipped" by students might have a bit of Drama Queen in them, as might students themselves who (as mentioned earlier) tend to inspire either very warm or very cold feelings from their peers. For that matter, a fulltime homemaker can also strive to stand out from the crowd in this way—by always being the PTA president, the Scout troop leader, and so on. In other words: Beware of showoffs.

For that matter, you might want to avoid getting overly chummy with someone you meet in a bar, given that that fun person drinking round after round while keeping everyone in stitches might well turn out to be someone you'd rather have avoided. At parties, this same kind of thing can happen. Yet it is also true that when a Drama Queen cannot be the star of the party—let's say someone else is more entertaining, or the guest of honor—the Drama Queen might instead be smoldering off to the side, ready to start bad-mouthing the party to the nearest available ear.

If you meet a new coworker who has this "star quality," pay attention to how other people who have known the person longer seem to respond. Someone who seems so full of life yet turns people off might just prove to be quite a handful. (If your boss is a Drama Queen, there will be little if any getting around it. You can put up with it or look for another job.)

There are plenty of people out there to be friends with or date, so there is really no need to bond with a Drama Queen if you do not want to. If you are partnered with one, you probably need professional help yourself to regain your dwindling self-confidence. But as such: You can try to minimize your run-ins with even intimate partners by giving yourself plenty else to do. Heck, you might even write a book or get a promotion at work as you drum up perfectly legitimate excuses to keep a safe distance.

As for having a Drama Queen relative: You can keep all contacts and visits to a minimum, period. It is very difficult to not get pulled into things when in the same room with Drama Queens, especially when you are connected by blood, and so you might just want to keep out of the mess altogether.

HOW TO END THE QUEEN'S REIGN

For all the difficulty they can cause, you might know a Drama Queen that you do not want to avoid. Maybe you work for or with someone who, for all their hysteria, still seems worth it. Or maybe that friend, relative, or partner still seems to have a great deal to offer, for all the ways they try your patience. Still, it would be nice to feel like your own life does not have to be lived at the mercy of someone else's latest crisis. So there are some things you can try to keep the Drama Queen at a safe, but not estranged, distance.

What is very tricky here is that Drama Queens tend to be all-or-nothing people. If you say to them: "I'm sorry, I'm busy now," they are likely to decide you have abandoned them forever, and write you off. In fact, on some level you might intuit that by saying this to such a person even once, it is a way of saying you want them to leave you alone.

Looking at the big picture, Drama Queens could benefit from getting more praise when they are *not* trying to be larger than life. You can say: "I enjoyed being with you today. It was low key and relaxed, and I liked that." If the Drama Queen manages to do a good job of listening to you, or makes you a decent hamburger, tell him so. Let this person learn that not everything has to be a Cinemascope production. Help him or her learn to trust the small, everyday moments of life.

Of course, you can only do so much for another individual. So when a crisis erupts, try appealing to the Drama Queen's sense of humor. These people do often laugh quite easily; it's just that they have trouble laughing at themselves in the throes of a so-called emergency. So give them plenty of attention, but try to get them to put things in perspective and be cognizant of what they are doing.

If the Drama Queen is relatively calm, you can also try getting him or her to talk about what is *really* needed, as opposed to the crazy stories being told to you. For example, you can try saying: "What's the real reason you called me at two in the morning? Are you lonely?" In this way, you can demonstrate that you are capable of caring about what happens to the Drama Queen, but at the same time you will not take any crap.

In Casual Encounters

If you are first meeting a Drama Queen at an occasion such as a party, things will probably still be in that very early, charismatic stage. So it might be a good time to start trying to normalize your relationship as much as possible by praising him or her for the small, normal, everyday qualities he or she possesses. If the Drama Queen is going on about what a mess everything is—signaling that it is your cue to help—see if you can lighten things up by joking about it. You might say something like: "Sounds like you should be on *The Young and the Restless*," or maybe even come right out with it: "My, we are a Drama Queen, aren't we?"

If the Drama Queen is simply being overbearing—so intent on being a star that you feel insulted or ignored—you can of course simply walk away, especially if the Drama Queen is obviously inebriated. But if you do want to take this person on, you can calmly and evenly say something like: "I didn't think that was funny. In fact, I thought it was cruel." At times, normalcy to a Drama Queen is like garlic to a vampire, and the Drama Queen will cower in the presence of your temperate and sane demeanor.

At Work

If a Drama Queen coworker is going on about his or her personal life, you can always use the classic excuse that you have to get back to your job. In fact, even a Drama Queen boss should understand this past a certain point.

If you know the boss or coworker quite well, you can once again try to turn it into a joke, or get at what their real needs might be. And still once again, remember to praise this person for the everyday things they do, such as performing their job well.

When a coworker turns Drama Queen over work related issues, you might want to keep a safe distance, lest you become associated in people's minds with such instability. However, if you must get involved, you can try getting them to snap out of it: "Look, we're all overworked. What makes you think you're any better than everyone else?" Once again, you are communicating interest and engagement in what the Drama Queen has been saying, while at the same time you are not letting yourself get swept away by it all.

A Drama Queen boss will need a lot of attention, whether you like it or not. Still, there is no need to become a human doormat. Besides, no matter how hard you try to attend to the boss's every need, sooner or later you will disappoint, and the boss might turn on you. So if the boss seems to be having a nervous breakdown because a report is five minutes late (or some such), try to calmly say: "Tell me what you want me to do." In other words, the Drama Queen boss needs to be reminded that you are there to work, not to be his or her nurse or shrink—but communicate this in a subtle way.

In Your Private Life

When you are intimately partnered with a Drama Queen—or even if you are extremely close friends—you should have license to tell it like it is. When the Drama Queen acts up, you should be able to say: "Look, I know you too well to believe the crap you're telling me. So if you want me to help, you have to be honest about what you're feeling, and what you need." You also should not feel that the relationship is one-sided, and you need to let the Drama Queen know that you have needs as well. Let the person know you appreciate the small things they do, perhaps even more than the big things. And don't be afraid to throw it back at them. Pretend to play a weepy violin, or applaud and shout "Bravo," when the Drama Queen gives a full performance. See if you can get him to own up to the BS he is trying to pull.

When a relative is a Drama Queen and you cannot or choose not to avoid seeing her, your best bet is trying to keep things light. Depending upon your personal connections with this person, it might not be your place to get her to open up on some deeply honest level.

As always, help Drama Queens realize that they do not have to make a big deal about everything, and sometimes it's okay to just be normal. Ask her to help with some tedious task around the house, and then thank her for it.

→ Drama does have a place in mental well-being. Drama therapy and psychodrama are used in a therapeutic setting to help people come to terms with their past actions and experiences. (But this transpires in a professional setting, with people whose job it is to listen.)

→ Both depression and addiction are associated with being an exceptionally needy person.

→ Overly needy people are at risk when it comes to longevity. Besides having proclivities toward substance abuse and depression, their relationships with others tend not to last, and long term, healthy relationships—intimate or platonic—are associated with longevity.

the know-it-all

CHAPTER SIX: Let's say you're having a pleasant Sunday brunch with friends. You're seated at an outdoor patio on a sunny spring day. In the middle of a sentence, you say something about how it feels warmer for this time of year than it usually does. A newcomer—some friend of a friend—begs to differ with you. "You're wrong," he forthrightly states. "I heard on the morning news that the record high temperature for today was in 1904, and that the high today would be five degrees lower than that. So it can't be *that* warm." A friend comes to your defense: "I'm sure all Betty [or Bob] meant was that it's a lovely warm day." But this other person is a Know-It-All, and cannot let the matter go: "To say it is *unusually* warm connotes exception, and five degrees below the record high could not by any stretch of the imagination qualify as an exception." He smarmily adds: "I suggest you go to the dictionary and look up the word, 'unusual.'"

Another friend says something about how really, this is not any sort of big deal, at which point the Know-It-All practically foams at the mouth and says: "It certainly *is* a big deal when people no longer know the meanings of common words in the English language!"

This may seem an extremely trivial anecdote, but that is the point. A Know-It-All is someone who cannot be wrong, no matter what. He or she must have the last word, even if the argument becomes convoluted—or even if it turns into an outright lie. Sometimes a Know-It-All feels backed into a corner. Someone has made a strong counter-argument, and the Know-It-All is on the verge of getting busted for Being Wrong. And so the Know-It-All says *anything* to win the little debate. In other instances—like the story above—a Know-It-All will pick a fight. It can be a small matter that no one else cares about, but unless everyone immediately acquiesces to the Know-It-All's point of view, he or she will fight it to the death. Spoiling everyone else's time matters naught. Supposedly, there is a principle at stake. And these so-called principles matter more to the Know-It-All than treating other people decently.

Now, there are many battles in this world worth fighting, and sometimes it is appropriate to let good manners take a back seat to defending what you think is right. But the Know-It-All is not really about principles at all. Instead, it is a personality trait that serves only to inflate someone's ego. The Know-It-All simply is scared to death of ever being wrong. And like any matter of life and death—even if only in someone's mind—stakes that high must be fought to the bitter end.

HOW TO SPOT A KNOW-IT-ALL

Unlike some difficult personality types, Know-It-Alls make little attempt to hide the way they are—even upon first meeting. Whether it be a stranger at a party, a boss or coworker, a friend, date, relative, or spouse, there is often a lack of subterfuge. Know-It-Alls *want* you to believe they really do know it all.

However, they ideally will start off on a personable, charming note, impressing you as they ever so generously and patiently explain to you what something or another is. Yet you might start to notice that they do not seem interested in drawing other people into the conversation so much as they want to lecture. Phrases such as "You made a good point" do not spring from their lips— excepting of course when they address the face they see in their mirror. Others tend to *ask questions*, rather than offer their own opinions.

Yet no matter what the occasion, if Know-It-Alls feel threatened they will not hesitate to defend their words at all costs. Disagreements are a normal part of life, but you cannot help noticing that in this instance, someone is fighting dirty. Rather than engaging in disagreement, this Know-It-All person is saying and doing whatever it takes to be in control. Ignoring here, lying there, throwing in an insult for good measure—you would think that the fate of the universe hinged on winning the argument.

You can spot Know-It-Alls in other ways, as well. If you say something like, "Boy, I'm having a bad day," other kinds of people might reply: "Gee, that's too bad." But a

Know-It-All is right there with answers for you—even though you never even asked a question. The Know-It-All knows *exactly* what your problem is, and what you need to do to fix it. It goes without saying that a Know-It-All's opinion is highly sought after; indeed, it is difficult to imagine how anyone manages to function without it.

There is a strategy common to many Know-It-Alls that you can watch out for. In football terms, it could be called the "Touchdown Fumble." A touchdown, of course, is when you score, and a fumble is when the ball is dropped, so the play is over. Know-It-Alls try to have both at the same time. They "fumble the ball," so to speak, when they are clearly in the wrong. Yet they seem to believe they can still "score a touchdown," even though so doing would be invalid. And so they make something up that sounds so ludicrous it becomes pathetic—you may not even know how to react, because you feel such anger and pity at the same time. And so on the surface of things, Know-It-Alls can convince themselves that they have scored another victory.

To use a fairly silly example, let's say a Know-It-All has just stated that the earth is a moon of the planet Mars. If it is pointed out in no uncertain terms that this is not true, the Know-It-All might reply: "Actually, scientists are saying now that it *is* true, because moons can also be planets."

Also be mindful of people who seem to never, ever admit that they are wrong. Some people tend to make excuses for themselves, but with Know-It-Alls, it is as though nothing wrong even happened. Your point of view, your sense of injury, simply does not have even one percent validity. They are right and you are wrong, period.

Know-It-Alls like to feel they have power, and so it is not uncommon for some poor office assistant to be designated to call you on behalf of the Know-It-All, whose voice you can hear in the background, telling the assistant what to say. Sometimes, Know-It-Alls will even go so far as to literally interrupt you by saying, "Stop." They seem to believe that you are so wrong and they are so right that by cosmic decree you simply must shut up and let the great Know-It-All explain what the *real* story is. Left unbridled, they will even deny you your right to any voice at all.

HOW DID KNOW-IT-ALLS GET THAT WAY?

Ironically, most Know-It-Alls actually are quite intelligent. After all, you wouldn't say you could play the clarinet if you couldn't, and you wouldn't try to pass yourself off as someone with a lot of smarts unless you believed you had them.

The problem is that most Know-It-Alls had reason early in life to doubt that they were as smart as they sensed they were. Perhaps the school environment did little to encourage their intelligence, or even put them down for asking questions or having ideas. Sometimes young Know-It-Alls ranked poorly in terms of standardized tests, were not put into advanced classes, or suffered similar indignities.

The home life, too, might have been one in which either little praise was given for being intelligent, you had to think or believe one way about everything, or else some other family member outshone the Know-It-All. Whichever the case, once again the Know-It-All grew up believing that he or she had something to prove.

Often by adolescence or so, Know-It-Alls begin to acquire a kind of cult following. They have a circle of friends (albeit even just neighborhood kids) who are rather in awe of them, and who tend to defer their opinions to them. Fledgling Know-It-Alls seem to say: "Forget about what the teacher said in school. I'll tell you what this really means." Their peers also learn that if they *do* disagree, the Know-It-Alls are likely to find this unacceptable, and will be right there with a clever retort designed to make further disagreement impossible.

Of course, there is a difference between being a clever thirteen-year-old and being respected for your mind out there in the grownup world. It is like the difference between being an acceptable high school musician or athlete versus making it to the pros. And so as they progress through life, Know-It-Alls find that others will in fact disagree with them—and maybe even trump them with claims that the Know-It-All cannot argue. Or at least not argue if the Know-It-All plays fair. And so he or she will resort to playing dirty, and saying whatever it takes to be technically "right."

In fact, over time, Know-It-Alls will develop all kinds of built-in strategies for pre-empting doubts from others. They often do not realize that others find them highly intimidating—but not in a positive, awe-inspiring way. It is more like: "So-and-So is such a pain, I'll just humor him [or her] and pretend to agree." Ironically, Know-It-Alls can win the battle but lose the war. First and foremost, they want to be taken seriously, and that is exactly what they lose over time. And on some level Know-It-Alls sense this, which of course only makes them angry, and increases their desire to control the conversation.

HOW TO AVOID KNOW-IT-ALLS

It is very difficult to get the best of a Know-It-All. When someone is incapable of admitting they are wrong . . . they will never admit that they are wrong! They will lie first, or insult you. No matter how much you tell yourself in advance: "If they say this, I'll say that," in the moment the Know-It-All will get the better of you 99 times out of 100. They *live* to be "right" and to "know everything," so they have much more practice and determination than you do. And so you just might decide it is best to avoid these people whenever possible.

Alas, it is rather difficult to avoid Know-It-Alls in terms of profession or pursuit. They can be found virtually anywhere. Obviously, career paths that are thought-intensive (such as universities, think tanks, politics, medicine, law, and the arts) will attract their fair share of Know-It-Alls. But you can also be part of a construction crew, and encounter a fellow worker who thinks he or she knows everything, and has all the answers to life's problems. You certainly should not let Know-It-Alls stop you from pursuing whatever career path you choose, so whether it is in the boardroom or at the fast-food restaurant counter, you can do your best to keep your conversations with these people to a minimum. Claim to be busy, remind everyone at the meeting that you need to get to the next item on the agenda, and in general avoid confronting them unless you are prepared to withstand insults and hurt feelings.

Highly zealous religious groups can also attract Know-It-Alls, who might find in the group the eager audience they have always been seeking. Armed with the belief that they are right while most of the world is wrong, they will then try to force family, friends, or even total strangers to believe the same way. Something similar can happen in other kinds of volunteer groups. Again, the answer need not be to stay away entirely, but to keep yourself—and the group—busy in other ways, so as to avoid these Know-It-Alls as much as possible.

If you encounter a Know-It-All at a party, it ought to be simple enough to excuse yourself. When a Know-It-All sits down next to you on an airplane (whereby you cannot simply change seats), and you would rather not have to listen to it, you can yet again express your need to busy yourself with other things. In general, be ready to encounter Know-It-Alls when it is just before election day, when you are in the lobby of a theater between acts, or when your company has brought in a so-called "expert" outsider—any kind of situation that might lend itself to exceptionally strong opinions.

If your family has relatively few college graduates—or maybe even just one—you can expect that some people will turn these higher-educated others into Know-It-Alls. The college graduate in question may or may not succumb to the temptation, however. If there are no college graduates, there still might be a relative who considers him- or herself extremely informed or well read, and will likewise try to show off. Or perhaps there is someone with an unusual career, or one that pays exceptionally well. Sometimes even just taking a vacation to an exotic locale can (at least temporarily) make someone into a Know-It-All, particularly in a family that tends not to travel.

When confronted with a Know-It-All relative, you once again might opt for the path of least resistance, and simply busy yourself elsewhere, or change the subject whenever possible. If you go out of your way to contact a Know-It-All relative to seek his or her advice, it is no one's fault but your own. If two or more Know-It-All family members get into a debate, you might be better off simply steering clear of it. Probably others will share your sentiment, and hopefully there is another room in the home to which people can excuse themselves.

If you are intimately involved with a Know-It-All and want to hold on to the relationship but do not wish to deal head-on with the problem, you can listen as needed, and then go on to something else. Friendship with a Know-It-All is probably less likely to survive, as there is less need for you or anyone else to stay in close contact with someone who gets on your nerves. But if you do want to stay friends, and you once again do not wish to confront the person in question, you can try to avoid topics that are likely to get the Know-It-All going. You especially might want to be selective in sharing information about yourself, as the Know-It-All might trample all over it and hurt your feelings without even realizing it.

HOW TO OUTSMART A KNOW-IT-ALL

Though avoiding the Know-It-All might often be the wise path, in some instances you might say to yourself: "Enough already. I don't care if he/she gets mad at me, I don't even care if I lose the argument, but I just have to speak up and let this person know that I can't stand it." As long as you are prepared to suffer some emotional wounds, then by all means bring it on. The wounds might well prove to be short-term, unless the Know-It-All plays an extremely significant role in your self. But oftentimes, all that results from these encounters is an ever-more defensive Know-It-All who is that much less likely to change his or her stripes.

A better approach is to begin by accepting the sad fact that the Know-It-All is beyond your help. Such deeply ingrained behavioral patterns—stemming from defensiveness—are unlikely to go away by taking threatening actions.

If you are willing to see this behavior as an unfortunate shortcoming instead of as a personal threat, you might be able to have a deeper and larger appreciation of the situation. And once you are in this other state of mind, you might be willing to try a few gentle tricks to win the Know-It-All over.

One strategy is to avoid making statements to them, and instead phrase things as questions whenever possible. Make the questions sound "innocent" and unbiased—a simple quest for the truth.

If it is strictly a matter of factual information that you are certain that the Know-It-All has just boggled up, you may ask something like: "I hear what you're saying, but now I'm confused. Because just the other day, I read in the dictionary [or newspaper, or whatever] that actually something else is true. What should I believe?" If your information comes through quietly yet solidly, the Know-It-All might be forced to do a deft about-face, and find a way to accommodate your information without seeming "wrong." Or, if the Know-It-All does stubbornly cling to his or her original version of the facts, bear in mind that others will pick up on this, and will think this person is a fool.

As for matters of opinion: Let's say someone has just told you that you cannot or should not think or do something a certain way for reasons that you can see are faulty. You can respond with: "Hmm, you do make a good point. In fact, that gets me thinking. What about the possibility of . . ." And then you can slip in, seemingly unnoticed, some other point that throws what the Know-It-All said into question. While there are no guarantees, it is *possible* that the Know-It-All, in an effort to save face, will then address this other point, finding it unavoidable but to make what you said seem to be what they themselves were saying all along.

In trying to pull this off, you should *not* expect Know-It-Alls to ever say: "You were right and I was wrong, I apologize." (Or if they do, then by all means buy a lottery ticket that day.) However, sometimes Know-It-Alls will simply start talking about something in a different way, and by implication you can conclude you got through to them.

In Casual Encounters

It should be fairly easy to take the low-key approach as described above when dealing with a casual acquaintance at a party or waiting room or bus stop. Try to frame it in terms of a question, and if the other person is unwilling to compromise at all, then it should likewise be easy to turn away.

At Work

In addition to the questioning technique, you can also consider swallowing your pride and yes, *flattering* the

Know-It-All. To maintain harmony with a coworker—let alone a boss—it can be useful to always preface your remarks by saying, "I appreciate all the hard work you do and your many creative ideas." You might want to especially pour it on thick in a written communication—and e-mails even more than letters. The written word can seem glib without a smiling face to back it up, and so a Know-It-All can feel especially threatened when something is put into writing.

Another form of flattery is to actually (gulp!) ask for the Know-It-All's opinion. Needless to say, the Know-It-All will be most eager to share it. However, if you once again try to frame it a certain way, you might be able to pre-empt certain kinds of answers. For example, if you do not want your boss or coworker to argue Point A, you can start the discussion by saying: "I respect your opinion because I know you are very informed on this. So since I'm sure we all know Point A will not work, what do you think we should do instead?"

In Your Private Life

These basic strategies of questions and flattery can carry over into your personal affairs. Still another tactic you might consider when you know someone on a personal level (whether as a friend, spouse, or relative) is to encourage them to apply what they do know a lot about to their own betterment—perhaps even the betterment of the world. Sometimes, of course, Know-It-Alls are quite successful (at least on the surface of things) in the career of their choice. But sometimes Know-It Alls are frustrated, wannabe scientists or politicians, and maybe they would be better off actually applying their need to be admired to something constructive. Saying this to a casual acquaintance might come across as smart-alecky, and saying it to someone you work with might be perceived as a threat—that you are telling her to get another job. But if it is someone you know well, perhaps it will be taken as a constructive suggestion.

Now, as you may recall, the Know-It-All is an extremely difficult type of person, even insofar as difficult people are concerned. And so it is possible that none of these approaches will work. You might ask a question, and get the very annoying answer you were hoping to avoid. Flattery might similarly get you no place. If such is the case, you are sadly left with little choice but to attack head-on (and be prepared to lose), or else detach from the person and situation as much as possible. Having a mini encounter group in which you explain how the Know-It-All is making you feel is unlikely to accomplish much. So at some point or another you might just decide to walk away, licking your wounds and awaiting a brighter tomorrow until this storm, too, passes over. You might take comfort in remembering that in the long run it is the Know-It-All who will lose out by alienating so many other people.

The tricky thing about Know-It-Alls is that on the surface of things they do communicate; unlike Brick Walls, they are willing to elaborate on whatever is being discussed. However, all their verbiage is aimed at blowing their own horns. You might think you can make some real progress with them, but your efforts may fail, especially if you are able to approach the Know-It-All in just the right way.

→ Studies have shown that being a Know-It-All might be related to narcissism. People with narcissistic dispositions are more likely to claim knowledge in areas in which they know little, if anything.

→ Being a Know-It-All is at odds with the nature of scientific inquiry. While some people think of scientists as "knowing everything," in actuality scientists first and foremost ask questions. That is why they are always conducting experiments—because they do not know all the answers. If you "know everything," you are incapable of learning any thing *new.*

→ Know-It-Alls can sometimes perform well in games such as Trivial Pursuit, or maybe even win money on TV for their general knowledge on a variety of topics. Online, there are literally millions of trivia games and tests. They may not know *everything,* but sometimes they do know quite a lot.

KNOW-IT-ALLS

the procrastinator

CHAPTER SEVEN: Everyone procrastinates from time to time. Maybe you keep meaning to write to an old friend, lose a few pounds, or repaint the living room, but you keep forgetting to make the time to do it. But some people seem to *always* procrastinate. And it's not just over small things. Getting them to do *anything* is about as likely as getting a goldfish to bark. They are like a walking and talking "To Do" list.

If through some cosmic fluke these Procrastinators actually do start something, they have this way of never finishing it. They paint *half* of the living room, and then leave the rest unfinished—probably with the paint cans out in plain view. Or they write half a letter to a friend—or fill out half of their income tax form—and leave it sitting unfinished on the kitchen table for countless decades. Or they sign up for a college class, but never finish it.

When Procrastinators live alone, their homes are usually a mess, because they cannot quite put away the groceries, take out any or all the garbage, or sort through their laundry. Even when Procrastinators make an ample salary, they might have a pile of "final notice" bills, because they put off paying them as long as possible.

If there were a place called Procrastination Heights, these people could all live together, and you could be spared the residue of their inability to start and/or finish things. (No doubt the town sign would read: "Welcome to Procrastination Hei—")

Alas, they live and work beside you, and so you must suffer the indignities of that half-painted living room, or wait *forever* for a coworker to finish an important report. Or maybe you are waiting—and *waiting*—for someone you hired to finally finish proofreading your thesis or landscaping your garden.

In some situations, it might be possible to simply do the work for the Procrastinator. But another delightful aspect of Procrastinators is that they often will vehemently insist on finishing whatever it is themselves. Moreover, the mere mention of the possibility that they are taking a tad long to finish painting the room or doing their taxes can render you all but accused of high treason. To hear the Procrastinator tell it, you are obviously the most nagging, controlling, stubborn, impatient person in the history of the universe.

It has been said that what matters is not the journey, but the getting there. However, Procrastinators take these wise words a bit too literally. They never get there at all, but instead prefer to turn painting the living room (or whatever) into a lifelong project. Michelangelo reached a point where he said, "Okay, Pope, let's say we call the Sistine Chapel finished." But for a Procrastinator, one's life work never reaches this stage of completion.

HOW TO SPOT A PROCRASTINATOR

Sometimes, Procrastinators give themselves away without even saying anything. One good clue is to take a look at where they live—or their desk at work. If it is a total mess, and there moreover is evidence (such as an old newspaper) that it has been a mess for quite some time, there is a good chance that you have made the acquaintance of a bona fide Procrastinator. A variation here would be if the person does not let you enter his or her home out of embarrassment over the mess. (Since Procrastinators are often very absorbed in their own private worlds, this might actually be an unconscious strategy to keep other people at arm's length.)

You can also pay attention to the things they say. For example, if on first meeting someone says they are thinking of doing something or another, and then on the second meeting no progress has been made, and then on the third or fifth meeting they are *still* just thinking about it, there is a chance that this is someone who tends to put things off. Do not judge too harshly—maybe there are good reasons for having put it off—but you still might want to keep your eyes and ears attuned to the possibility that you have encountered a Procrastinator.

For that matter, if the person tells numerous stories about how numerous people are always getting on their case to do things, there might well be a pattern here. Sometimes one or two people might unfairly hassle someone, but if virtually everyone is "nagging" the person in question then maybe the problem is with them and not everyone else.

If the person lives alone and tends to be unkempt or disorganized in appearance, it could be because he or she tends to put things off until the last minute. If the person has a partner—and apparently this partner is a fulltime homemaker or in any case dotes over their mate—appearances can be deceivingly pleasant. It might actually mean that a Procrastinator has someone who picks up after them. So pay attention to comments about how they couldn't do it all without their partner. Likewise, in a work situation an assistant or secretary might spend an inordinate amount of time in the care and feeding of the boss.

It is *not* indicative of a true Procrastinator to dread or put off a single task. So if a new acquaintance says something like: "I keep putting off telling my daughter she can't have a puppy for her birthday," go easy on this individual. But if it turns out the reason why the daughter can't have a puppy is because Daddy never got around to buying one, he might be a Procrastinator, after all.

Sometimes, too, a new person in your life might seem quite interested in getting to know you—whether as a friend or something more—and yet when you suggest a movie or a walk in the park, the person will respond vaguely: "Um, I think I'm probably busy." Now, it could very well mean that you have misread this person. But it is also possible that he or she simply has trouble making *any* sort of commitment. You should not try to force the issue; respect the other person's need to be vague and noncommittal. Still, you might find solace in the notion that maybe it is nothing personal against you.

HOW DID PROCRASTINATORS GET THAT WAY?

There is an important distinction to be made when it comes to Procrastinators: Some people outgrow their tendency to procrastinate in their teens or twenties, while for others it becomes a lifelong pattern. So if, for example, a high school or college student tends to have trouble finishing homework, it might just be a phase—a function of being young. Of course, it is nonetheless in the young person's best interests to in fact finish his homework, and the problem should not be ignored. But it can be useful to bear in mind that such a young person is hardly unique.

Quite often, genuine lifelong Procrastinators grew up in extremely critical environments. Their families (and maybe also their schools or churches) were perfectionists who seemed to always be saying that whatever the person was doing, it could have been done better. Parents or other authority figures do not always mean to be such a defeating influence, and may not be aware of how nag-nag-naggy they come across. In fact, quite often the children keep their resentments to themselves because despite their anger and frustration they do not wish to hurt the grownup's feelings. Over time, the child starts to accept the message as normal, and internalizes that creepy voice that says, "No, you can't," or "No, you're doing it wrong." And after awhile a kind of mental paralysis sets in.

Sometimes Procrastinators become what might be called "closet perfectionists." Underneath their seemingly blasé indifference about getting things done, they are as sharply critical as their families were. Procrastinators may *seem* not to care, but underneath it all they actually care so much that they are afraid to do anything.

These are often the kind of people who puzzle others, because they seemed to have "so much potential" but they never seem to go anywhere or do anything. Sometimes, they even have trouble holding down a job—or looking for one—and might instead opt for never leaving home, or finding someone to take care of them. If they do work, their place of employment probably expected much more out of them than they eventually got. When they set up their own business, it will probably be difficult to sustain, because they do not make all the phone calls or what have you to truly get it moving.

In other instances, Procrastinators can grow into "passive-aggressive perfectionists." Once again, they harbor a nagging inner voice that makes them unable to commit to doing things, but it takes on a more seemingly helpless character, as if not-so-secretly wishing that someone else will come along and do it all for them. These people signal that they need help. They are highly disorganized and seem barely able to remember their own names. If someone suggests that they make a list of things to do in order to be more organized, they will either utterly freak out that you are being such a dictator, or else keep a million different lists around the house that add to the chaos. Such Procrastinators simply feel overwhelmed. While others can say, "Okay, I have a lot to do today, so first I will do this and then I will do that," these people are unable to logically prioritize.

These passive-aggressive sorts either flail about or else stumble upon an occasional rescuer. But of course, it may not really be in their best long-term interests to be rescued, because all it accomplishes is the perpetuation of the same cycle. They also tend to bungle things with rescuers, who will lose patience with them over time.

Procrastinators can also exhibit an inability to concentrate on any one thing for very long. Sometimes this can mean that they suffer from ADHD or some other affliction, but it also can simply be a fancy way of not having to commit to anything.

HOW TO AVOID PROCRASTINATORS

As exasperating as Procrastinators can be, they usually mean no harm. They might even deserve your sympathy, because underneath it all they want to do the "right" thing. Still, if you highly value qualities such as order and punctuality, you might be better off keeping these people at arm's length whenever possible.

When meeting someone at a social event, or on a first date, be mindful of those who seem to have considerable trouble making up their minds about which cheese to sample, or where to sit in the movie theater. (If, that is, things have even progressed to where the person has actually left the house.) Such indecisiveness could mean the presence of a grade-A Procrastinator.

If you're hiring someone to rake your leaves or move your furniture, do not be shy about asking for references. Find out in advance if this is someone who tends to get the job done promptly. Also, if something is normally done by a team of people, be careful about hiring anyone who claims that they can do it all by themselves, probably for a cheaper price. It just might mean that the deal literally *is* too good to be true—and things that should take a week to do take a month, and so on. Some people flourish when self-employed, but for others it is simply a way of avoiding having other people "tell them what to do"—i.e., be made to finish the job they started.

If you are a high-energy person, you might want to avoid low-energy work environs. For example, you probably will not be happy working in a small shop in which everyone sits around all day. Extra-long coffee breaks or lunches are nirvana for some, but for others it can mean that this a job that will prove very unsatisfying, and the people you work with might not like you, either, for being so "uptight" or a "workaholic."

When you work at an otherwise satisfactory job and a coworker is a Procrastinator, perhaps the problem will take care of itself—i.e., this person's days of employment will be numbered. But sometimes these people hang around for years. They will not only take their sweet time finishing their own work but will also sabotage the efforts of others. This is done largely to insure that they themselves will not have to do anything new, or anything extra—or in the final analysis, do much of anything at all. If you work side by side with such a person, you might decide to take the path of least resistance, and to avoid her as much as possible. Believe in what you are doing, and work around the Procrastinator as if building a house around an old tree.

If your boss is a Procrastinator, hopefully there is a boss at the next level who is not. If you work for a small business and your boss always puts things off, you might just want to keep your options open and look for another job, because it is possible that the business is not destined to last long. When there are other levels to the organization, you might elect to just go about your business, and make sure you are doing *your* job. This makes it more likely that if anyone gets in trouble, it will be your boss and not you.

When a close friend is a Procrastinator, you could decide to make a lot of plans that do not involve this person. Certainly you can avoid asking such a person to plan a camping trip or even a night at the movies. When possible, you might want to invite others to whatever it is, so that at the last minute you are not stuck having to do whatever it is alone. Or, failing that, simply be mentally prepared to do it by yourself—or not do it at all.

Being intimately involved with a Procrastinator can be dicey, because there can be a lot of squabbles over messy houses, unfinished projects, the other person's general lack of drive, your "nagging" ways, and so forth. If you feel the good outweighs the bad, you might choose to simply accept the Procrastinator for who he or she is. Count on her for little if anything, get what companionship you can get from her, and live your own life.

Similarly, when relatives are Procrastinators, do not accept their offers to trim your hedges or install your new home theater—unless of course you are so afraid of hurting their feelings that you would rather feel frustrated and angry. To avoid ill feelings, you can plan around these people as much as possible, making sure that nothing hinges upon their showing up or getting something done by a certain date.

Whatever your relationship to the Procrastinator, if something you need done is not getting done, you might just want to take a deep breath, and quietly take whatever it is elsewhere. If you want to avoid a scene, see if you can arrange this with minimal prior knowledge on the part of the Procrastinator. Have all the pieces in place, instead of saying: "I'm going to be looking for a new contractor." For if you say something like that, the Procrastinator is likely to insist that he or she be given another chance.

HOW TO GET PROCRASTINATORS OFF THEIR YOU-KNOW-WHATS

Procrastinators will not respond well to criticism. They will think you are nagging them, and this will remind them of their crummy childhoods—which will of course only increase their inner fear, and make them even less able to function. Also, if you go on about how bad they are making you feel, Procrastinators will feel guilty (even if they do not show it), and will likewise try to avoid the issue. Remember, since they are capable of doing much more than they do, they probably have wasted their energy and intelligence on finding ways of wiggling their way out of these predicaments. However bad they are at finishing things, they can have a lot of charisma or smarts when it comes to avoiding blame.

Whether Procrastinators come across as ultra-indifferent or as utter scatterbrains, they can benefit from some gentle encouragement and subtle direction. True, you cannot change them and they must change themselves; there are no guarantees that you can help. But as difficult personality types go, Procrastinators are one of the more approachable ones. Since they do not like to commit to anything, even their anger is probably not all that scary, and they are more likely to retreat within themselves than anything else. So with the right approach, some real good might actually happen.

In general, you should keep things as specific as possible. Focus on the task at hand, rather than the character defects that indicate to you that the Procrastinator needs professional help. Such might well be the case, but it is doubtful that your words will be taken to heart when you are being so critical. So try to instead get the Procrastinator to take a good healthy step back, and see the situation at hand as a series of small, calm, common sense actions. Often, Procrastinators aim too high—they want perfection or nothing. So if you can help them to approach their situations more realistically and less judgmentally, you might actually help them to finish what they have started.

In Casual Encounters

If a Procrastinator is doing a job for you, you can try to

break it down to a short list of manageable steps. Meet in person when possible, as over the phone you will have less control over the situation. In today's world, e-mail can come in handy as well, because you can list precisely what needs to be done by when.

If the person you have hired is being mysterious about exactly what is taking so long, ask nonjudgmental questions: "I'm curious: What is the first thing you need to do at this point? How long will it take? What is the second thing you need to do?"

At Work

If you want to take a more proactive role when dealing with a Procrastinator coworker, be prepared to play a lot of political games. A direct, insulting approach will once again only make the other party defensive (even if they do not show it). And since it is not your place to be lecturing a *coworker*, you might even get in trouble for it. So again, subtle works best. See if there are "innocent," blameless ways in which you can have deadlines created or enforced. Do not name names, but instead discuss how because of some unavoidable fact of life, does not the such-and-such project need to be finished by such-and-such a date?

The Procrastinator might try to stop you by prolonging discussion on something, re-introducing it after a plan has already been set in motion, or raise other, phony issues aimed at dragging things out. If this is the case, you probably will have to do a lot of wheeling and dealing behind the scenes. You will want to make sure that you have the support of the key supervisors or advisors. It will be best if you do not come across as hateful or complaining; be as tactful and positive as possible. Perhaps you can approach it without even mentioning the Procrastinator by name. As long as those in charge say: "You're right, this needs to get finished, so you have our support," go ahead and do what you need to do. Present a constructive plan that is hard to disagree with. Unlike Brick Walls, Procrastinators will retreat fairly easily, so there is even a chance that the Procrastinator will avoid the meeting or final vote.

Obviously, you should not tell your Procrastinator boss what a lazy good-for-nothing he or she is. But what you can do is respectfully ask what you can do to help finish whatever it is, when does it need to be done?, and so on.

In Your Private Life

Whether someone is a friend, relative, or intimate partner, you might be able to help them get over their procrastinating ways—but once again, not by criticizing. Instead, see if you can help them to see how getting the job done need not be such an ordeal if they break it down into small steps. Help the person see that with a little bit of organization, the project need not feel so impossible. This should be especially easy when it is something that does not personally involve you or your own goals. Praise them for what they do get done. If the Procrastinator can scale down his or her goals to a manageable level, good things can be accomplished. For example, perhaps the Procrastinator can give up on totally rebuilding the house and instead be satisfied with building a new patio. And perhaps most important of all, let them know that they do not have to be perfect to have your respect and affection.

→ Procrastination can be caused by, as well as cause, depression. People who feel inadequate or disconnected are more likely to feel depressed, and thus less likely to want to do things. At the same time, when people have little to show for themselves, they are more likely to become depressed.

→ Some research has indicated that about 70 percent of college students experience bouts of procrastination.

→ Even outside of college, moments of procrastination can happen to most everyone. There are studies that suggest more than 90 percent of our population will procrastinate from time to time, and for as much as 20 percent of our population it will be a serious problem.

PROCRASTINATORS

the snooty snob

CHAPTER EIGHT: Everyone is a snob—yes, even you. Whenever you say, "No thanks, I deserve better than Brand X," you are being a snob. You are saying that what other people might settle for is not good enough for you, thank you very much. If people never wanted more than the mediocre or common-place—be it for themselves, their loved ones, or their communities—no one would advance in this big, bad world, and life would be much less interesting. The problem is not with being a snob, but with being a Snooty Snob. That is to say, someone who does not simply have healthy high standards, but is actually mean-spirited about being superior. The Snooty Snob *has* to be better than everyone else. And he or she will make certain that everyone thinks so even when it means insulting others, or hurting their feelings.

Whatever Snooty Snobs say, it has this funny way of indicating how vastly superior they are. Not that they like to argue, or even necessarily talk at great lengths. But what they do say will probably be aimed at creating a distinction between them and you—namely, that you belong worshipfully at their feet, kissing the hem of their garment. On rare occasions they may encounter someone worthy of their attention, and so will try to monopolize this person, as if to further send the message that only the best is good enough for them.

When they are not tooting their own horns, Snooty Snobs are likely to turn all but silent. Friendliness is not exactly their middle name. Since Snooty Snobs are *so* superior to you or me, it is a small wonder that they seldom find it in themselves to bother with the usual little niceties of life. Unlike mere mortals, they need not return greetings of hello, ask how you are doing, engage in token compliments, or even say thank you. For all their snootiness, they can have downright bad manners—if indeed good manners stand for courtesy and respect. But Snooty Snobs have no intention of getting to know you as an equal. Indeed, you should consider yourself quite fortunate that they even so much as acknowledge your existence.

Some difficult personality types would not be happy to know that they are making people feel bad. But with Snooty Snobs, making you feel bad is entirely the point. While encounters with them are probably not as volatile as with Brick Walls or Big Bullies, they share with these other types a desire to win at all costs, and putting you down is more of a minor inconvenience than anything else. Since they do not say much, when in doubt the Snooty Snob can simply walk away from the whole thing.

HOW TO SPOT A SNOOTY SNOB

Snooty Snobs are easy to identify at parties or other kinds of social events. They are either off by themselves, sending out a haughty, do-not-come-near-me vibe, or else engaged in conversation with probably one other person in a manner that indicates no one else can join the little huddle. Their back is turned to you; if you do approach, they make no effort to draw you into the conversation. Probably the person they are talking to is someone considered relatively "important," given the occasion; Snooty Snobs are not likely to monopolize the attention of a wine waiter. If it is a family gathering, they are probably talking to the matriarch or patriarch, or the one doctor or lawyer in the group. In a roomful of Hollywood celebrities, the Snooty Snob will single out the most important film producer or movie star.

Oddly enough, the exception to the rule is likely to be an event given in honor of the Snooty Snob. You are then more likely to find him sitting in a corner of the floor, talking if not to the wine waiter then someone's grandmother or eight-year-old nephew—the most dramatically *unlikely* person for him to be talking to. Why? Because once again the message is that Snooty Snobs are not like everyone else. You cannot figure them out, meet their needs, or even get their attention. They need not trouble themselves with talking to everyone as an equal, and will circumvent having to do so with this most conspicuous display of fake humility.

Essentially, Snooty Snobs use a similar strategy whether meeting you at your cousin's wedding or on the job. For example, when you ask someone if they watched a certain TV show last night, a Snooty Snob is likely to disdainfully say: "No, I only watch PBS." Now, there is nothing wrong with watching PBS—or for that matter, enjoying the opera, or appreciating gourmet food. But Snooty Snobs use these proclivities to let you know how immeasurably superior they are. It's one thing for someone to say they only watch PBS because they refuse to pay for cable. But it is another to show scorn for people who do watch more popular forms of TV—or like Top 40 music, or indulge in junk food. People who are truly secure within themselves will admit to partaking of guilty pleasures from time to time—even when they are rich and famous, serious artists, or renowned gourmets. Instead of saying they only watch PBS, such people will say something more like: "No, I've never seen that show. What's it about?" And if they *did* actually watch it, they will admit it. The thing about Snooty Snobs is that sometimes it isn't even true that they only watch PBS, they just want everyone to think it is.

Cliché though it may be, another way to spot a Snooty Snob is to trust your gut instinct. If a new acquaintance is making you feel very self-conscious or much less comfortable than you normally are in social situations, there is a fairly good chance you are in the company of a Snooty Snob.

HOW DID SNOOTY SNOBS GET THAT WAY?

Some Snooty Snobs are as rich as their haughty attitude would seem to suggest—but they can also be dirt poor.

Flipping the coin over, there are rich people who are *not* Snooty Snobs. Whether rich, poor, or in-between, Snooty Snobs share in common a need to seem superior. Some would call this a superiority complex—while others would say it is really an inferiority complex. However you want to look at it, the upshot is that Snooty Snobs grow up feeling that they need to prove something. Perhaps they felt that they were less favored than a sibling—or they came from the poor side of a rich family, or even though their family was rich it was lacking in some other way. Maybe the father was always drunk, or they grew up without a father—there was *something* that other kids had that they did not have. A variation on the same theme would be that some other kid in school won a coveted honor that the Snooty Snob wanted, or maybe this person was not accepted into the college she most wanted to attend. And so the Snooty Snob grows up with a sense of being Avis in a world that prefers Hertz—the perennial runner-up, the second choice, the glorified loser.

At the same time, Snooty Snobs also get a sense that other people do not like them very much. Maybe there is something to this. Kids can be cruel, and maybe the Snooty Snob was the only kid not invited to a birthday party, or told outright by other kids to stay away because they did not like him or her. And so the Snooty Snob starts to show off against this basic insecurity. Like Scarlett O'Hara vowing to the radish that she will never be hungry again, so do Snooty Snobs reach a point where they say: "I will never be humiliated again. Maybe people will not like me, but I will not let the hurt show. I will be haughty and indifferent, above it all, as if I could care less." Thrown in for good measure is a defensive rationale that the reason people do not like the Snooty Snob is because no on else is refined enough to appreciate his or her fragile, unique specialness.

People, of course, tend to like those who seem genuinely engaged in their company, and Snooty Snobs seem far more engaged in their own selves. And so people tend to keep their distance—which makes the Snooty Snob that much more haughtily defensive, and so people stay all the farther away.

Yet at least some of the people some of the time will express a certain awe toward the Snooty Snob, and in the absence of genuine affection, this might be taken to be genuine affection—or at least better than nothing. So the Snooty Snob does get at least some validation to keep on snooting away. People often like Snooty Snobs best upon first meeting them, because there is less of an awareness of how utterly self-absorbed they are, and how put down they will make you feel. But after awhile, the Snooty Snob will say to him- or herself: "It's their loss, not mine," and find other people to superficially impress until the spell wears off.

HOW TO AVOID SNOOTY SNOBS

You might remember the old joke that goes: "Pretentious? *Moi?*" There in a nutshell you have the world that the Snooty Snob inhabits. By all means go to that trendy new restaurant or experimental art show, if that's what rings your chimes. But do not be surprised if such locales seem to attract a disproportionately high number of Snooty Snobs. If you have an exceptionally low threshold for these kinds of people, you might want to at least make sure that you have a number of down-to-earth companions to join you.

By the same token, you are less likely to encounter Snooty Snobs at that dinky little mom-and-pop restaurant that has great food at low prices and is one of your town's best-kept secrets. As a general rule, when people are genuinely enjoying themselves, it tends to repel Snooty Snobs, like so much citronella against mosquitoes.

But you do not have to be at an upwardly mobile event to encounter a Snooty Snob. Even a beer bash at Joe the mechanic's might play host to someone with delusions of grandeur—though such a person is unlikely to stay long. When you are confronted with a Snooty Snob at a party or a similar event, by all means feel free to walk away. The Snooty Snob probably wants you to, anyway.

As for jobs, Snooty Snobs are likely to avoid situations that do not afford them at least the fantasy of moving up in the world. At a university, for example, a secretary will not be "promoted" to a professor or dean. Yet at a private corporation, perhaps today's secretary may be tomorrow's executive. So you might find more Snooty Snobs in lower-level positions at workplaces in which they feel they can hobnob with the upper echelon. And what the company does can also be a factor. A Snooty Snob is more likely to be drawn to a company that imports rare works of art than one that makes rubber bands.

If you have a date or are making a new friend, be mindful of the kinds of activities they suggest, the names they drop, or the places they talk about going to. If there is *never* anything down to earth about the conversation—if it is all pretension and affectation—then you might just want to move on. Snooty Snob relatives need not be invited over or contacted often—in fact, it is unlikely they will contact you, so you need not feel guilty.

Should you be partnered with a Snooty Snob, you will probably be made to humor this person a great deal. Still, you can work to insure you still have your own life independent of trying to endlessly impress others. Keep up at least some friendships or activities that you genuinely enjoy. Also, suggest activities with your spouse that are simpler and more down to earth. It helps here to look for the Snooty Snob's Achilles' heel—that is to say, is there some kind of junk food or ordinary activity that even the Snooty Snob admits to liking? If so, make an offer that your partner cannot resist.

HOW TO GET A SNOOTY SNOB'S NOSE OUT OF THE AIR

As difficult people go, Snooty Snobs can be relatively easy to deal with. This is not to say that they are never exasperating. But given their tendency to keep people at arm's length, they are seldom truly dangerous, and so you can feel relatively safe about trying to hang in there with them.

Snooty Snobs often take it for granted that they will not be well accepted by others. Their air of superiority is often just so many sour grapes, a buffer against the rejection they are sure will come. So these people are always mindful of the possibility of leaving the room, leaving the relationship—of having to walk away in order to save face.

Therefore, if all you want is to make the Snooty Snob go away, that should not be hard to do. You can look the person in the eye and say something like: "Your fake sophistication fools no one," or "Nobody likes people who think they are better than everyone else." But saying these kinds of things can be unnecessarily cruel. Snooty Snobs may make you feel uncomfortable, but they usually are not evil, despite what would seem to be a streak of sadism in their personalities. It is not so much that Snooty Snobs enjoy making you feel bad as much as it becomes the only way they think they can feel good.

Believe it or not, you might just try reaching out to the Snooty Snob in your life. Given their tendencies toward grandeur, these people are often good in a crisis, so if you are confused or upset you might be surprised by what a sympathetic listener this normally unfriendly person is. You might have to endure a condescending lecture, but probably the Snooty Snob will give more indication of caring than you thought was possible.

Even if you have no urgent problems, try inviting the Snooty Snob to join you in something social. (You might get turned down the first time, so try one more time before giving up.) Go for something in between low and high rent. For example, the free night at an art museum, or a free concert in a park, can appeal to both the snobbish side of the person and also suggest something more carefree and ordinary. There are movies that get good reviews *and* are crowd pleasers.

You can guide the Snooty Snob into the world of humanity, helping him or her to feel the pleasure in sharing everyday activities. Share a little gossip. Eat some gooey fudge. Let the Snooty Snob know that you really like him or her as is, and that extra layers of embellishment are not necessary.

In return, you might be delightfully surprised by how smart and engaging Snooty Snobs can be, once they come down off their high horse. They actually do have some original observations, and however pretentious some of their proclivities might be, some sort of good taste probably did rub off on them. They might have sage advice about what to serve at your dinner party, or how to handle an unusual situation.

At the same time, remember that this is someone who is used to spending a lot of time alone. So the Snooty Snob in your life might at times have a short attention span, and abruptly seem to lose interest, or end an evening early. Try not to take it too personally. As long as the person is friendlier again next time, he or she probably deserves another chance.

A word of caution: If you reach out to a Snooty Snob, you *will* get put down sometimes. The Snooty Snob will be unable to resist making a sarcastic wisecrack or disdainful criticism that makes you feel a bit foolish. If you find this unacceptable, then by all means point it out to the person—and if the problem persists, move on. But you also might try beating the Snooty Snob at his or her own game, and coming right back with a similar putdown. After a time or two, the Snooty Snob just might back off.

In Casual Encounters

If a Snooty Snob is standing off to the side at a social event and you would like to talk to this person, try a bit of flattery. For example, if you find this person attractive, you can say: "I've been wondering if you were just going to stand here all night by yourself, looking so terrific." Or you can suggest a conspiratorial chumminess: "I can see you're a lot like me. You think this party is pretty awful, don't you?" If you get the brush-off after making these gallant tries, then the Snooty Snob is probably beyond hope, and pat yourself on the back for at least giving it a try.

If the Snooty Snob is snubbing you by keeping you out of a conversation you would like to enter, once again flattery might get you somewhere. You can say: "Pardon me, but if I may interject, I really like what you just said. In fact, it reminds me of something I've been thinking about that I'd like to get your opinion on . . ." If these types of remarks do not succeed in lightening things up, again, chalk it up to the Snooty Snob's jerkiness, and move on. (It is also possible that the Snooty Snob had too much to drink in order to survive being in a crowd, in which case you should probably stay away altogether.)

At Work

When a coworker is a Snooty Snob and you would like to feel more of a connection, you can try reaching out to the person—and gently putting him in his place—as already discussed. Additionally, perhaps it is possible to suggest a joint project—if not specifically about work, then mutually planning a surprise party for someone else in the office. However, if none of this seems to work, you cannot just walk away, as you would from a stranger at a party. And so you might want to simply ignore it all whenever possible, changing the subject or pleading a need to return to what you were doing as needed.

If you do want to respond to their snooty words and deeds (and trying to be friendly clearly did not work), you need to remember that you are after all on the job. Underneath it all, the rift between the Snooty Snob and yourself is probably relatively unimportant. Still, if you feel the need to get in a couple of digs now and then, you can try feigning utter disinterest in whatever the Snooty Snob is bragging about (such as by yawning). All this will only make the Snooty Snob feel that much more disconnected—but again, if being friendly didn't work and you feel you need *some* release, at least keep it subtle.

If your boss is a Snooty Snob, you can look on the bright side. You might appreciate the fact that he or she does not want your attention every second of the day. And at least the road to flattering the boss is clear; you know that "all" you have to do is make lots of compliments. If he or she is going on about how they had some sort of French something or another for dinner last night, it is simple enough to ooh and aah about how worldly your boss is, and how delicious it sounds.

You should probably not bother your Snooty Snob boss with your personal woes unless you know each other quite well—and in any case, do not use work time proper to do so, but come in over your coffee break, making it clear you are not using company time. Also, flattery will help. Say how the boss seems like someone who would be very understanding. But what might work better is showing your boss how to relax. Bring the boss homemade cookies, for example.

In Your Private Life

As already mentioned, there is a way to make friends with a Snooty Snob that just might prove a happy arrangement for all concerned. It is a friendship that will probably require maintenance from time to time as you remind the Snooty Snob to cut the crap, but you may well feel that it is worth it.

If you are partnered with a Snooty Snob and want to stay together—and also want to engage in more than the diversionary tactics previously mentioned—it probably will not do much good to talk about how inferior you are made to feel. It might not even help to say your feelings are hurt. The "sick" part of the Snooty Snob might just find all this music to the ears, and the result will be a greater sense of fake power and grandiosity. Hard as it might be in the moment, you are better off trying to reassure the Snooty Snob that you do care, and that he or she does not have to prove anything.

When a relative is a Snooty Snob, you can try offering the basic cocktail of friendship and mild putdown. Since you are related, the Snooty Snob might feel compelled to give things a try with you, even if in other arenas of life such would not be the case. At the same time, be aware that family is often at the root of someone's snooty snobbiness, and so it might well be extremely painful or difficult for the Snooty Snob to even be in attendance at a family event. In fact, it could very well be that the Snooty Snob is often conspicuously absent from this or that family event. In spite of yourself you might even find yourself worrying about this person, and even (yes) wishing he or she was there.

➔ Snobbery can take many forms. In the United States, there can be *regional snobbery*, in which Northeasterners believe they are the superior species—but then, so do Southeasterners, Westerners, Southwesterners, and so on.

➔ Snobbery is associated with introspection and critical capacity. If properly harnessed, snobbery can aid in making sound, honest decisions.

➔ It has been speculated that cult groups sometimes recruit by appealing to a snobbish side of people's nature—some people will enjoy believing that they are privy to the alleged one great truth of life, while other people are not.

the temper tantrum type

CHAPTER NINE: Some people freak out at the drop of a hat. They yell and scream, they run out of the room, they slam doors, and they call people names. What these Temper Tantrum Types get across is exactly what they got across when they were five years old: That if they do not get their own way, something bad will happen. They can be complimented on their steadfast consistency of purpose. They promise something bad, and boy, do they deliver it.

People who easily become emotionally unhinged might well benefit from medication, and should be encouraged to seek professional help. But sometimes, it is not so much a matter of needing medication as it is being manipulative. Sometimes, people *could* control themselves, but choose not to in order to elicit certain responses from others.

What is it that these people want? Obviously, one thing is attention. They want it made known that their feelings or needs are not about to be ignored. Sometimes it even goes a step further, in that they want you to worry and fuss over them—even if they snap your head off for trying. And they also very much want to get their own way. Hopefully—and quite often—if they freak out loudly enough and long enough, others will relent, thinking, "Okay, okay, anything is better than having to put up with this." And so Temper Tantrum Types strive to have their proverbial cake and eat it, too. They get lots of attention, *and* they get to say, "Screw you, I want what I want."

The bad mood of the Temper Tantrum Type has a way of taking over the entire setting. It moves in like a rain cloud over everyone else's parade. Roll out the red carpet—the Great So-and-So is displeased. If Drama Queens want to be stars, Temper Tantrum Types want to be dictators.

Temper tantrums are absolutely normal in toddlers. Unfortunately, for some people there is a carry-over effect into the adult years. People well beyond the legal age of consent carry on as if they need a diaper change. Well, they need *something*, all right, but you are way too polite to tell them what it is.

Nonetheless, the problem still has to do with communication. The Temper Tantrum Type knows of no other way to communicate displeasure than to make it everyone else's business. They expect that by pulling a big scene, everyone will acquiesce. And often, they are right. Even when they technically do not get their own way, they still have communicated that they are no one to mess with. So it becomes less likely over time that anyone will stand up to them, out of fear of causing another outburst.

HOW TO SPOT A TEMPER TANTRUM TYPE

Temper Tantrum Types can be very charming upon first meeting. In a way, they are overgrown children, so just like five-year-olds, they might make an effort to ingratiate themselves. People who think nothing of freaking out in front of others must have a certain confidence, and so they are not shy about introducing themselves and getting to know people. They often invite you out to dinner, and in general communicate a sense of, "Let's be friends."

What you might want to pay attention to are their emergent biographies. There are probably some dramatic empty spaces in their lives—close blood relatives they have not seen in years, or a "best friend" whom they have only known for a few months. Like so many rolling stones, Temper Tantrum Types gather little if any moss. People (or sometimes jobs) tend to come and go. They often have a string of different spouses, or have one with whom things are on again–off again. If single, it probably will not be for long, because they will want to latch on to *someone*. In fact, they might naively move in with someone after barely making their acquaintance. When Temper Tantrum Types remain single, their friends should expect a lot of "desperate" phone calls.

While no one gets along with everybody all the time, these Temper Tantrum Types will have *a lot* of stories about how they had it out with this or that person at work, or how in a bar someone picked a fight with them. Yet oddly enough, they may have trouble admitting that they have any problems, and register genuine surprise when you suggest that they are ill-tempered or overly emotional. Again, like children, part of them thinks they must always "make nice," and so they find it hard to admit that there are people they do not like.

Also, if the topic of mood-altering medication comes up, a Temper Tantrum Type might reveal that they have tried six or eight different kinds. Failing this, they might express an extremely unsympathetic viewpoint toward the idea of people being medicated—they will go on about how people must work these things out without any "crutches." Perhaps you happen to agree, but with Temper Tantrum Types this is often a defensive ploy.

Once you see this type of person *way* overreact to something—maybe someone cuts in front of them in the supermarket line, and you would think that the world was coming to an end—expect it to happen again. This will be especially true when they all but tell you it is: "I'm not like this much anymore." Or what can be even more disconcerting, afterward they may pretend as though nothing even happened.

HOW DID TEMPER TANTRUM TYPES GET THAT WAY?

Some years back, it became fashionable to talk about having an "inner child" inside you—some part of yourself that had been neglected for virtually all your life that still need-ed basic nurturance. But when it comes to Temper Tantrum Types, it might be more apt to talk in terms of having an inner spoiled brat.

Temper Tantrum Types are often the subject of special attention as children. They might have been an only child, the child of divorce, or for one reason or another inclined to make the parents or other primary caregivers guilty. Or maybe the child's entire existence was aimed at proving how wondrous the mother or father was. Whatever the specifics, those who raise him or her feel inclined to sub-mit to the child's every whim. Such children are not taught much about limits, and remain convinced that whatev-er they want, they should have. When they pull a scene—even as teenagers—the parents never say, "Cut it out, you're embarrassing yourself." Instead, it is still a matter of: "What's wrong, honey?"

As children, they might be envied by peers with less indulgent parents. Temper Tantrum Types are seldom made to accept whatever the teacher said or did, because Mom-my or Daddy will be right there giving the teacher holy heck. As much as it is desirable to have proactive parents who defend their children, it can be taken too far. Some-times, children need to learn that they will lose, that life can be unfair, and that it is best to let things go and let other people have their way—that you do not *always* get what-ever you want. But Temper Tantrum Types are never taught that lesson. The parents feel it is a bad reflection on them if their child loses out in any way, shape, or form—especially when the parents have some other reason to feel guilty.

Temper Tantrum Types are another example of how to win the battle but lose the war. People might well give in to them because they are such a pain. But there is real scorn and cynicism behind the way that Temper Tantrum Types are humored along through life. Of course, the Temper Tantrum Types want very much to be taken seriously, and might sense that such is not the case—that people treat them kind of like a crazy person. And so this makes the Temper Tantrum Type feel more frustrated and misunderstood—which leads to further outbursts.

HOW TO AVOID TEMPER TANTRUM TYPES

If you happen upon someone pulling a fit, you might want to just keep on walking—unless of course there is a real chance that someone will get hurt, in which case (quite seriously) you are better off calling the police or 911. If you think that you have some sort of magical powers to soothe the insanity, then physician, heal thyself. Whether it be a stranger at a bus stop or a party, or even someone you know, one of two things is likely to happen: Either you will get your head bitten off by the Temper Tantrum Type, or (in some ways worse) this person will come to rely on you, which will be the last thing you want. Unless of course your idea of a happy life is having someone calling you at all hours of the night because they had to give someone a piece of their mind today and you are privileged enough to hear all about it. It can seem very flattering—at first—to have someone lean on you in this way, but sooner or later you will disappoint the Temper Tantrum Type, and when that happens, look out. You will learn all too well that you were not immune to this person's raging bad moods, after all. Surprise, you are only human.

If a new acquaintance flies way, way off the handle over something, there is a good chance they will do it again five minutes or five days later. If the person apologizes afterward, it is perhaps a step in the right direction, but there are no guarantees that they will have a better grip on their emotions next time around. Once again, do not assume you will be immune from all this; sooner or later, you are likely to be the nearest available target.

If you truly want to avoid this type of person, you might want to stay away from certain kinds of work settings. A potential downside of careers that seem "interesting" and permit a great deal of individuality of expression is that they can attract more Temper Tantrum Types. This can mean working in show business or the creative arts, or even hospitals or law firms that pride themselves on having the great So-and-So on board. Such people can prove to be extremely spoiled and temperamental, and act as if they are so irreplaceable that they can pull a scene whenever they feel like it if it means getting exactly what they want. Sometimes, too, small businesses are started by someone who simply wants to be complimented a million times a second, and figures that by hiring underlings this will be the case. If such fails to be the case, the owner might feel that he or she is "entitled" to act out, since after all who signs your paycheck? (Which slight detail you will not be permitted to forget for a moment.)

In clubs or volunteer groups, be mindful of a tendency for one person to dominate, as if it is really Bob or Betty's group and not whatever it is supposed to be. If the other group members act like fawning disciples, there is a good chance that they are really in a kind of denial over how much they are letting this other person's bad moods call all the shots. Also, of course, be mindful of things that other people say about this person, even if veiled in politeness: "He certainly expresses his opinions," or "Be careful how you say that to her," are not exactly what you'd call good omens. This would also apply to work settings—see if your coworkers put on or take off their kid gloves around a given person.

There are other clues to look for at work. If the atmosphere itself tends to be quite well organized, there is probably less of a likelihood of their being a Temper Tantrum Type. Granted, there might be other problems associated with it, but if the company functions like a veritable well-oiled clock, probably it does not tolerate or inspire a great many emotional outbursts. Where there is chaos in the workplace—or even the boss or coworker with piles and piles of disorganization surrounding them—there is a greater chance that someone is going to fly off the handle.

The nature of the work can of course also be a factor. If the tasks being performed are either low-key (a compact disc store, for example) or matters of life and death (such as the emergency room of a hospital), the people involved are probably able to keep their emotions in check. Easygoing work environs simply do not lend themselves to such outbursts, and in emergency situations people are much too focused to freak out. It is more the mid-range of tasks—such as extremely busy offices in which the handling of forms can take on greater cosmic significance than it accurately deserves—that Temper Tantrum Types are likelier to be a part of. Also, jobs that require a great deal of teamwork are also less likely to tolerate irrational outbursts.

Turning to more intimate contexts, you probably already know if a spouse or a close friend or relative is a Temper Tantrum Type. A new friend or date might act out, and then apologize later—as already discussed. You might want to think twice—if not a third time—before letting this person get too close. A relative whom you cannot totally avoid can still be kept at arm's length if you keep a safe distance. Make encounters as brief as possible; take your sweet time responding to letters or e-mails, ultimately apologizing (if need be) for being too busy to get back sooner.

GETTING TEMPER TANTRUM TYPES TO ACT THEIR AGE

If you want the Temper Tantrum Type in question to remain part of your life, one thing you can do is set a good example. Show them how you yourself handle problems in a reasonable and even manner. (If sometimes in the past you have *not*, then use this opportunity as a good excuse to take your own behavior up a notch in the maturity department.) The Temper Tantrum Type needs to learn that it is possible to express disagreement—even sadness or anger—without going ballistic. And it is possible to enjoy another day of life without necessarily getting your own way.

Another strategy is to briefly and succinctly point out a reasonable solution. For example, if the Temper Tantrum Type is freaking out because their relatives never send them a holiday card, you can say something like: "Maybe you should send them cards yourself, then, to get the tradition going again. If you don't know what to say, just sign 'love,' with your name."

If it turns out that the Temper Tantrum Type *has* been sending cards without getting any in return, try reminding this person that these kinds of things happen to people all the time: "Ouch, that does hurt, doesn't it? I go through that myself with my sister-in-law." Then change the subject, or end the phone call, as need be. Keep it a *small* problem, a minor irritation that is part of life, and hey, what can ya do?

Should the Temper Tantrum Type be genuinely scaring you, do *not* think you can just la-de-da handle it on your own. If he or she locks the bathroom door and refuses to come out (as if to plant the fear in you that something desperate might happen), go ahead and call 911—within earshot of the Temper Tantrum Type. If you get a desperate phone call from a Temper Tantrum Type, you can say: "Your problems seem to need much more than I can give, so I am calling the local twenty-four-hour crisis center on your behalf," and then get off the phone and do it.

In less extreme situations, do not hesitate to say: "I have a lot of other things I need to get to, and while I hope it all works out I do not see what good can come from dumping all this on me. If you are that upset at Marsha, then you need to talk to her yourself. Call me and let me know how it goes. I *care*, but I do not want to get caught in the middle." Or as a possible variation: "You and I both know that Marsha is impossible to deal with, so I strongly suggest that you just let it go."

In other words, you want to communicate that while you do like this person, whatever "crisis" is happening is not about to overtake your life. If the big scene happens spontaneously in your presence, you again need to look at the matter pragmatically: What is the Temper Tantrum Type freaking out about, and what is a fast but reasonable way of finding a resolution to it? You might need to begin by firmly stating that the tantrum needs to stop, and it needs to stop now. You can even say: "Look, I'll get you a glass of water or a cup of tea or some aspirin, but you need to stop this right now."

You can then try to once again keep the focus specific, offering practical solutions. Get out a pad and pencil, if need be, and make a step-by-step plan of action. Have as much of it as possible come from the Temper Tantrum Type. If you disagree, offer subtle suggestions: "Yes, that might work—unless of course you want to instead try it this other way?" You see, the Temper Tantrum Type must learn to rely on his or her own ability to rationally and calmly fix things. Moreover, if it seems like you are dictating what he or she should do, you will either be resented or—even worse!—be thought of as a savior.

If the Temper Tantrum Type insists that this is something that cannot be resolved so easily, or simply pouts and refuses to cooperate, then try saying something like: "Look, I am doing what I can to help out here. I know you feel bad. So do I, about a lot of things. It's the best I can do, take it or leave it."

Once the matter seems under control, you might even want to say something about how you do not like it when this happens: "In the future, please make more of an effort to calm yourself around me. See a doctor if you need help in handling your emotions, but I don't want to be around this anymore." If the Temper Tantrum Type accuses you of abandoning him or her, try saying: "You're wrong, I do care. But I have limits, too, and all this takes a toll on me, too. Please get some professional help, because I can't do this anymore."

In Casual Encounters

Probably the most proactive you can be if a casual acquaintance is acting out is to find someone who knows him better, and have her take care of it. If things look truly serious, you can always call 911. But there is probably little if any reason to involve yourself in someone's tantrum when you do not even know the person well.

At Work

When a coworker pulls temper tantrums, you might consider going to your supervisor and requesting that something be done. If it would appear that such is not possible, or trying backfires and makes matters worse—then if you otherwise really like your job you can grin and bear it as best you can. If you are extremely confident about your position at work, you might try rolling your eyes and saying. "There he/she goes again," the next time it happens, and see if you can get things to move on. But you do not want to say or do anything that escalates the problem—you want to be thought of as someone who contributes to the peace and not to the conflict.

When a boss is a Temper Tantrum Type, you have your work cut out for you and then some. You can cope better by remembering that you are ultimately doing it all for yourself—that it might well help you get ahead (or at least feel very secure about your position) by babying your boss as needed. Also, as a subordinate, a lot of the issues at stake probably do not affect you the same way they would if you were an equal, so you can play babysitter and congratulate yourself for being such a sane person. However, also bear in mind that today's savior can be tomorrow's pariah if you let down the Temper Tantrum Type by claiming that you have some needs of your own to take care of. If you are truly being abused—if you feel like your whole life is consumed with the care and feeding of your boss—you might need to set some ground rules, or look for another job.

In Your Private Life

Should you be close friends or partnered with a Temper Tantrum Type, you hopefully have a fair amount of leeway to express how you feel about the whole thing. If the relationship is totally one-sided—if your own needs are ignored—you should consider counseling or else ending things. But if indeed there are good times that outweigh the bad and at least some of the time the Temper Tantrum Type is there when you need him or her, you can once again try to keep things in perspective by reminding the person that the situation at hand might well be solvable by taking small steps. You also will have the advantage of being able to administer either platonic or romantic TLC in so doing, to help smooth things over.

Still another approach that might work is to firmly and succinctly throw it right back at the person. Should the Temper Tantrum Type slam the door in a huff, you can slam the door right back. If he or she starts screaming about how you don't really care, or what have you, you can say that you feel the same way—albeit in a calmer tone of voice. This might help the person sober up quickly, and return to a more adult frame of mind.

When some other kind of relative is a Temper Tantrum Type and you cannot avoid being exposed to the latest extravaganza, you can still keep the emphasis on solving the situation: Does the person need 911, can it be resolved in small, common-sense steps?, and so on. If all you get for your time and trouble is more temper tantrums, then calmly let the person know they are upsetting you, and take a firm step away from the situation.

→ If you think being in a bad mood can help you win a game, think again. Considerable evidence in sports psychology suggests that players train and concentrate best when they are in a good mood.

→ Emotions tend to follow thoughts. If you can train your mind to disassociate from negative assumptions, your feelings are less likely to turn negative.

→ It is not enough to suppress your anger. Suppressed anger has been associated with high blood pressure, hypertension, and some forms of depression. Instead, it is important to redirect your energy from the inside out—taking the mental and physical steps to truly calm down. Do some deep breathing, take a hot bath, and eat and sleep properly, besides training your mind.

TEMPER TANTRUM TYPES

the two-face

CHAPTER TEN: Unless you have lived your days in a black hole in space, you have more than likely encountered a Two-Face. When there is disagreement between two or more people, there often is a third party who says this to this one and that to that one, and makes everyone think that he or she is on their side. Now, maybe you are the kind of person who can see both sides of an argument, or you try to play peacemaker between warring parties. Perhaps, yes, you have even indulged in a bit of gossip now and then. But none of this is the same thing as being a Two-Face. It is as if these people have no conscience or principles at all. They get a weird adrenaline rush from stirring things up. At the same time, they strive to insure that everyone likes them, so they say or do as needed to convince you that you have their 100 percent loyalty—only to behave similarly moments later with someone from an opposing point of view.

In a way, the Two-Face is a variation on the Brick Wall. Instead of feeling like your words are totally ignored, it is more like you can feel your words getting poisoned somehow as the Two-Face turns them into fresh fodder for whatever is going on. Though superficially these people can seem quite pleasant, you often leave conversations with them harboring a sense of dread or discomfort. Your gut instincts are telling you this is not someone to be trusted, and unless you are a certifiable paranoid your gut instincts are probably right on the money.

Even when your original bone of contention involves something the Two-Face said or did, it will get all twisted around so that other people are involved, and soon you have issues with all sorts of people over all sorts of things. The Two-Face is extremely skillful at staying out of the line of fire, and will not hesitate to insure that your protests become directed at someone else. Two-Faces think nothing of stretching the truth or lying outright to keep things the way they want them: Everyone else is all but ready to kill everyone else, as the Two-Face looks on with delight. "Gossip" is their middle name. Soap operas feature many a Two-Face character; unfortunately, real life can seem like a living soap opera when a Two-Face is hanging around. There might well be conflicts in your life anyway, yet oddly enough they have a funny way of dragging on or even escalating when a Two-Face is involved.

Even when there is nothing tangible to dispute, their drive toward self-preservation will hamper any kind of meaningful progress or resolution. For example, Two-Faces think nothing of telling Republicans that they themselves are Republican—only to tell Democrats that they are Democrats two minutes later. This is not about "being polite," because if you do not think it proper to discuss politics you can always change the subject. Two-Faces are so concerned with having everyone's confidence that they never take a real stand.

HOW TO SPOT A TWO-FACE

Two-Faces are often overly eager to ingratiate themselves. They laugh a bit too long or hard at the end of an amusing anecdote, they are overly interested in hearing about your job, and they may well express an inappropriate degree of interest. For example, they might offer their phone number and say to call them if you need someone to talk to, when all you said was that you weren't sure if you were happy with your new computer. For you to like them, they feel they need to do what they did as children—agree with you, and listen and listen. Their empathy can seem flattering, but something about it might seem too good to be true. And indeed, there will be strings attached down the road as the Two-Face comes to seem less like a friend and more like a troublemaker. Plus, you want your friends—let alone your intimate partner—to have some substance. You may not agree on everything all the time, but when someone does nothing but agree with you it starts to seem unreal—as indeed it is.

Sometimes, they will start to say they did not like a certain movie or type of food—but then when you register the opposite opinion, they will quickly change what they were saying to agree with you. There also might be a noticeable tendency for this person to contradict him- or herself across situations. A third party might say that the Two-Face claimed to share a particular taste or opinion with them, only to have expressed a different point of view the other day with you—one that, coincidentally enough, was in alignment with your own worldview.

When confronted, Two-Faces often claim to not remember the earlier conversation with you, or will insist that you had it all wrong, or that the third person did. They will say just about anything but the truth.

You also might notice that Two-Faces, despite what they claim to believe, do not get into the same kind of normal disagreements that you do. Let's say you are a staunch Democrat. In a roomful of Republicans, you just might elect to respectfully disagree. But the Two-Face—who claims to also be a Democrat—will instead be getting along all too peachily with the Republicans. Or it can be the other way around, if you are a Republican. The main thing is that the Two-Face might seem at first to be the kind of person who "gets along with everyone." But after awhile, you start to see that it is really just that the Two-Face is afraid to take any risks at all with anyone.

Sooner or later, it will come to your attention that this seemingly wonderful new friend or coworker is blabbing all sorts of stuff you confided to them, or telling other people about things you did that you simply assumed would be kept private. The Two-Face was not your special confidant after all, but was playing both sides of the fence.

HOW DID TWO-FACES GET THAT WAY?

From time to time, it is perfectly normal to take the path of least resistance and simply agree with someone. And you might well find yourself unwittingly in the position of having "stereophonic ears" as one person at work (or in your family) confides one side of an argument, and another person confides another. We all must sometimes engage in a kind of juggling act as we try to take actions that hopefully offend as few people as possible. But Two-Faces are insecure people who are excessively afraid of not being liked. They want to be all things to all people—and like the old saying goes, this means they end up being nothing to anyone.

Two-Faces often grow up in households in which they feel they have no license to express their own opinions. Maybe the entire family was dogmatic, or maybe there was a powerful sibling or parent who wanted to control everyone's thoughts, opinions, and tastes. Whenever dissenting viewpoints were presented, Two-Faces were ridiculed, or perhaps even punished. Also, if a close family member was a substance abuser, mentally unbalanced, or suffered from a long physical illness, there might have been an unwritten rule that no one should ever challenge this person.

Adding to the mix, the school environment probably also encouraged super-conformity. Any idea or question that was not part of the daily lesson was squelched mercilessly. Only fanatical agreement with the teacher led to good grades. Sometimes, too, a religious or other kind of group can serve a similarly negative function.

Another common situation is for the Two-Face to be

confided in inappropriately as a child. Warring family members—be they older siblings, parent and grandparent, or parent and parent—will dump all their grief onto the innocent ears of a child. The Two-Face is hearing both sides of the story, and knows of no way to react other than to keep listening.

Thus, the Two-Face comes to believe that only by seeming to agree with everyone all the time will they have any connections to other people. Of course, such connections are actually quite superficial, because there is little that can be counted on as genuine. But what *is* genuine is the Two-Face's intense desire to be liked by others, which translates into never ruffling anyone's feathers. The Two-Face believes that if he or she disagrees, it will cause an argument—which will in turn cause the other person or persons to abandon the Two-Face forever and ever. Something nameless and irrationally "bad" will happen if the Two-Face expresses an honest opinion—let alone if he or she informs the other party that their arch enemy just got done similarly confiding in the Two-Face.

In school, Two-Faces similarly learn to be on everyone's side at once. They tell both kids running for class president that they have their vote, and then keep their fingers crossed that they do not get caught in the complex web they are weaving. Occasionally, of course, they *do* get caught, and there might be a brief period of repentance—especially as they get older and their duplicitous ways are causing real harm. But probably this makes some people genuinely angry at them, and so Two-Faces might become even more afraid of upsetting people. And so despite the new honest behavior promised, Two-Faces remain as dishonest as ever.

Just as children can graduate from candy to alcoholism, so can Two-Faces add a dangerous dimension to their repertoire as they get older—they not only pretend to a sympathy they do not have, but they also start to gossip behind your back. What you tell them gets told to your "enemy," and vice versa. Even if the enemy does not start out in such a role, the intensity of the gossip will be such that relationships tend to deteriorate, molehills become mountains, and friends become ex-friends, and lovers ex-lovers.

HOW TO AVOID TWO-FACES

Some people are able to take Two-Faces with a grain of salt. For such people, Two-Faces are harmless or amusing or simply weak and cannot help themselves. But if you have been genuinely stung by a Two-Face and wish to avoid encountering another such person in the future, there are certain situations you might want to avoid.

First, obvious as it sounds, if you know for a fact that someone is being a mole—that she is consorting with the enemy, and then delivering dispatches to your side—do not be surprised if she cannot be trusted. You may think that ultimately such a person is on your side—but you might be tragically wrong. Be mindful as well of people who *love* to gossip. If you think you will be excluded from their reports to others, you are simply being naïve. For that matter, people who seem a bit too much the peacemaker in the midst of a volatile situation might well prove less than saintly. Maybe they do not want to bring people together so much as they want to toy with everyone's mind in order to avoid the crossfire themselves.

When Two-Faces are what might ironically be called "lucky," they are able to apply their deceptive natures to occupations that can get them ahead. Any enterprise that requires an inordinate amount of sucking up is likely to attract a fair number of Two-Faces. This can include sales positions, exceptionally aggressive small businesses, or anything to do with show business, the arts, or high-profile sports—anything in which you might need to tell one person one minute that they are the greatest, and then say the same thing a second later to someone else. But while some people consider this a necessary evil they must perform to put food on the table, for others it is as natural as breathing. In fact, they are unable to turn it off, and treat everyone in the same phony-baloney way.

Even in other kinds of occupations, be aware of people who seem overly agreeable, and who are always trying to get you to confide in them. The same would hold true when it comes to dating a new person, making a new friend, or meeting your in-laws. This does *not* mean that the moment someone dishes someone else or seems to relish a gossipy anecdote he is dangerous. Virtually everyone gossips from time to time. But some people do it without any sense of loyalty or viewpoint. They simply switch from one side to the other.

HOW TO GET A TWO-FACE TO DROP THE MASK

You can avoid Two-Faces when possible, or you can choose to tolerate them for who they are—or you can try to get them to treat you with more honesty. As always, you cannot expect to radically change another person, but here you might be able to encourage them to at least some of the time make different choices.

One thing you can do is to make it plain to the Two-Face that you do like him or her, and so it really is okay to disagree with you. It is not necessary to like *all* the same movies or foods in order to be friends with you. And while religion and politics can of course make for intense disagreements between people, sometimes people with differing views can agree to disagree, and be close despite their differences. So even if this person truly does believe differently on important issues, perhaps you can still be part of each other's lives.

Of course, there can be a problem here, in that the Two-Face, underneath it all, might have no real idea what to think or believe. He or she is so used to just going along with someone else that there seems to be little genuine feeling for anything. What Two-Faces therefore might need is encouragement to make a more positive use of their chameleon-like natures, and read a lot of different books and ask a lot of different people questions. In the meantime, they need to learn that it is also okay to say: "I don't know what I think."

You can also set a good example by demonstrating that while you yourself sometimes suffer disagreements with others, it does not destroy you. It is possible to compartmentalize these moments, and still have a nice day, and a nice enough life. And while a little bit of gossip is unavoidable, you can make it clear that you do not wish to talk about

So-and-So behind her back. Even if this person is someone whom you really would like to gossip about—a boss who fired you, or an ex-spouse—the cost of so doing with a Two-Face might be more than you are willing to pay. The Two-Face is likely to use it against you, and tell that former boss or ex-spouse that you were badmouthing him or her.

If it comes to your attention that the Two-Face has in fact proven to be disloyal, and you have other reasons for not wanting the Two-Face out of your life, you can have a short, succinct conversation about how you feel. Do not get too accusatory; it will only make the Two-Face more afraid. But you can calmly explain how hurt and betrayed you feel, and that you therefore will not be confiding in the Two-Face anymore.

In fact, you yourself need to get over a naïve assumption that a Two-Face is completely loyal to you when you know for a fact that they regularly communicate with the "other side." Someone who just had lunch with the boss who fired you is obviously *friends* with the boss, so of course the two of them talk about you behind your back. So in these situations, it is probably best to avoid certain topics of conversation. You will have more peace of mind over time, and the Two-Face can once again be reminded that it is not necessary to play these sorts of mind games in order to be in your life.

In Casual Encounters

If you meet this kind of overly eager person in a social setting, and you feel that in many ways this is someone you would like to get to know, you might want to establish some ground rules right away. Say right up front that you do not like to gossip very much, and do not care to badmouth the host. If asked about your favorite food or movies—let alone your politics or religion—ask the other person for *his* opinion. In other words, if someone seems to be all but dissecting you, turn it around to find out more about this other person. When a Two-Face is being super-nosy, you can always say: "I don't see why you need to know this."

If you end up turning this person off, then so be it. She will at least get a sense that you are not someone who enjoys being manipulated. And at best, maybe you can still make it plain that you want to get to know this person anyway, and that the usual mind games are not needed with you.

At Work

Bonding with a Two-Face coworker can cause serious problems. As the old saying goes, you will be judged by the company you keep. Others might come to regard you as being a similar kind of gossipmonger. You also might well find yourself having less time to get your work done as you become increasingly embroiled in whatever crazy scenario the Two-Face is helping to generate. Still, if for whatever reason the Two-Face is someone you will be working with closely—or in other ways you like this person—you can once again make it plain that there are certain boundaries not to be crossed.

In a work environment, it should not be difficult for someone to grasp that you do not want to get involved in a certain situation, or even comment on it. Even the world's biggest Two-Face should understand that people are often very careful about what they say or do at work. Do *not* kid yourself into believing that if you preface your remarks by saying: "Don't tell this to anyone, but . . ." that the Two-Face will actually keep it a secret. Their behavioral patterns are far too ingrained.

If a Two-Face coworker does start to gossip or pry, and you are tired of simply excusing yourself, you might try saying in as nice a way as possible: "You know, Bob, I like working with you, but I really am uncomfortable when you try to pry into my personal life, or get me to say something bad about Sally."

When you are concerned about getting caught in the middle of something, do not go running to Sally to explain your side. Instead, send a coworker you know you can trust (or even an outside friend) an e-mail that documents what happened. If later on you need to prove that you did not really say whatever it was about Sally, you have dated proof.

Should your boss be a Two-Face, you can try looking on the bright side. Sooner or later, either the boss will get fired for making one too many messes—or else will get promoted, and in a different way be out of your immediate sphere. To some extent, it might seem wise to side with your Two-Face boss—but unless this boss has truly unquestionable power, you might be hitching your wagon to the wrong pony. Sometimes bosses *are* replaced, particularly when they offend enough of the workers.

You are better off once again establishing parameters. Most bosses will understand that you do not want to talk about So-and-So—even if the boss wants you to—and that it is not part of your job description, you have a lot of work to do, you want to be careful, and so on. If you become good friends with your boss, and there is someone at work whom everyone pretty much agrees is a jerk, so be it. But this of course is not the same thing as being part of a Two-Face's intricate games.

In Your Private Life

If you are friends with a Two-Face and would like to remain so, but would also like to feel less involved in his or her mind games, you once again can try to steer things in a different direction. Change the subject as needed, and do not share anything you do not feel comfortable sharing. If you know that the Two-Face has in fact used your friendship as fodder for others, but you want to give the person another chance, make it clear that this type of behavior is not acceptable. You can say something like: "I enjoy our friendship, but you like a certain level of intrigue that I am not comfortable with. I don't appreciate your telling other people the things I tell you, so it must stop." If the Two-Face tries to deny having done so, remain firm that you know it happened, and that it must stop—and then leave it at that. You probably do not want to go on and on about how bad it made you feel, because that opens the door to more gossip.

In other ways, you can continue to let the Two-Face know that for you, friendship is not about badmouthing other people, and that the Two-Face can *relax* with you and just be friends. If it reaches the point where this is no longer true, the Two-Face will probably sense it—such people are often shrewd—in which case it might well signal the end of things. But if the Two-Face cannot be honest after being given several chances to be so, then you might be better off being friends with someone else.

As for dating or cohabiting with a Two-Face, the basic strategy is again to set a good example, and let the person know that with you it is different, and all that pretending to agree is not needed. And still again, you have the opportunity to communicate this positive message in romantic ways you would not do with a friend. You can also make it clear how hurt you are if and when the Two-Face betrays your confidence.

When an unavoidable relative is a Two-Face, probably other family members are well aware of this. You should be able to find ways of protecting each other, and agreeing not to get into it all with this person. When you do have to associate with the Two-Face relative, try to take it all with a sense of humor. Do not get into it with this person; listen politely as needed, and say, "Thanks for sharing," and then go on about your way.

→ Some people might assume that women are more likely to be Two-Faces, since according to the stereotype, women "love to gossip." But actually, men are just as likely to talk about people behind their backs. It is just that men tend to not recognize that what they are doing is gossiping, and call it something else.

→ Research has found that often when someone talks about someone else, the audience will assume that the speaker is the same way. In other words, when you gossip that So-and-So spends too much money, the person you confide in might conclude that you do as well. So your gossip might come back to haunt you.

→ In intimate contexts, deception often hurts more than the act itself. People are more likely to forgive their spouse for unfaithfulness per se than for the fact that they were lied to.

TWO-FACES

be not too hard

EPILOGUE: It's been fun to take a look at the different kinds of difficult people, and how to find ways of coping with them. As you go back out into the world, keep in mind a few other things.

First, try not to be too hard on people. No one is perfect, most of us try our best, and we all need each other. You should not be some total masochist who never stands up for yourself. But if you are *always* avoiding this person or trying to correct that one you will miss out on a great many pleasures that life has to offer—even, yes, in the company of a difficult person. Where there is humanity, there is difficulty. While you can learn to handle difficult people more effectively, you will always encounter *more* difficult people in the future. So you might as well get used to it. 'Tis the nature of the beast called life.

Also, remember that even difficult people have their good qualities. A Big Bully, Big Mouth, Brick Wall, Constant Complainer, Drama Queen, Know-It-All, Procrastinator, Snooty Snob, Temper Tantrum Type, or Two-Face who is working with you instead of against you might prove to be an invaluable ally. Today's archenemy might be tomorrow's best friend. So do what you need to do, but keep an open mind.

Finally—and this is the hard part—take a deep breath and consider the possibility that maybe, just maybe, from time to time *you* are a difficult person in someone else's life. Reading this book, you might think, "My brother Charlie is such a Know-It-All." But maybe as far as Charlie is concerned, you are one as well. Others can make our lives difficult, but then, so do we ourselves. Playing the blame game will not get you much of anywhere. A life without forgiveness and understanding isn't worth much. Just as you would want others to get past your transgressions toward them, see if you can find it within yourself to do the same.

Whatever challenges fate places in your path, may you enjoy the journey.